The Baby In
The Biscuit Tin

Kathy Lavelle

chipmunkapublishing
the mental health publisher

Published by
Chipmunkapublishing
United Kingdom

http://www.chipmunkapublishing.com

Copyright © 2014 Kathy Lavelle

ISBN   978-1-78382-087-0

Chipmunkapublishing gratefully acknowledge the support of Arts Council England.

The Baby In The Biscuit Tin

For Michael

Kathy Lavelle

Chapter 1

A baby's screams shook the building and I leapt from my narrow bed.

"Tommy", I screamed. But Tommy was cast away in the darkness far from this place. The screeches were coming from further down the corridor, blood-curdling sounds which threw me into a panic. I sat on the narrow bed holding my head on my knees, rocking and sobbing. My room was up in the tower, in the northwest corner with a small window and a view across the whole countryside, hills and harbour. The door to all my past life had been slammed behind me. For a while I heard nothing but an eerie, frightening noise in the steeple.

There were earth-piercing cries of wailing women in the night, hurried footsteps and angry, unintelligible exchanges between nurses and patients. Where were the loving arms that had always been there to comfort me when I woke in the night?

There was only the wind across the moor and down to the sea, shrieking an eerie song over some neglected tombstones, tombstones without names. In a frenzy I wiped a mass of sweat from my face with my nightgown. I got on my knees and wept uncontrollably. My body was bathed in sweat and a pang of fear went through me.

This was a scene from my own book, not yet put down on paper, but written deep in my consciousness. I couldn't read or write then. You could call me illiterate. Father kept me at home to help on the farm and each time I returned to the village school I was chided for my backwardness and often got the cane or was left standing in a corner holding up my blotted copy book. After a year or two, I stopped going altogether.

"Be quiet," an angry voice yelled from further down the building.

There were sounds of footsteps in the hall, angry voices and then stillness. I found out later about the tranquillisers. This brought a ghostlike stillness over the place and later, how much later I have no idea, I came to myself with a start. I was alone and I could hear no clash or cries, only the sound of a low moaning from another room made weirdly hollow by the wind. How long this lasted I have no idea for a blankness took over. In my sleep I relived the events of that first day when I was handcuffed and dragged from my home.

The small group stood in silence outside the farm door.

"We have to do this," Fr. Lynch's voice still thunders in my ears. "There is no other way. You are a danger to yourself. You need treatment."

"I am the most dreadful, shameful failure," I thought. Night fevers conjured up all sorts of visions with high walls around, threatening to curse me, doors bolted against the world.

I was looking at a life that was bound to be spent alone in this place without intimate companionship but I just wanted to be with my family, to hold my sister, to feel Nana's warmth around me.

I was overtaken suddenly by memories of Tommy. It was a pain so deep I felt it through my whole mind and body. My eyes were swollen, with red blotches on my cheeks and neck. That night everything had lost its meaning. I only felt a longing, a loneliness and a great loss. Gradually I slept restlessly as the wind squalled and rattled the slated barns in the farmyard. It was a long night. Every night was long. The days were long.

"What was my crime?" I asked myself this question over and over again.

"How had Fr. Lynch been allowed to decide my fate?" He was the judge, the jury and the prosecutor.

In my nightmare I saw Uncle Johnny, lips curled with contempt as he grabbed me and pushed me down despite my pleading. Afterwards I crawled through dark shadows between the thick heather branches. My forearms bled from the scratches but I felt no pain. I just had the urge to run and run forever.

I would spend my life paying for a hideous crime that someone else had committed.

Chapter 2

My hands were tied hard behind my back.

"You'll be back," Nana said as she squeezed me close to her warm body.
I could feel her heartbroken sigh.

"I have stitched something into the hem of you dress," she whispered.

Nothing will ever be as painful as those last moments on the doorstep. Nana stood there to say her final goodbyes but father grabbed her roughly and pushed her into the house. I imagined I could see her thin face through the small bedroom window but, handcuffed, I couldn't wave. I nodded and did my best to smile. Looking around trying to see her, shapes and shadows swam before my eyes and soon the window was out of sight. That was the last time I ever saw her. I had tried my best to remain cheerful for her sake but when we rounded the bend I burst into heartbreaking sobs..

The van accelerated smoothly taking me away. I looked out of the window and through my tears I watched the trees and fields and sky melt and merge into each other in a passing blur. The sun would never shine on my life again. As we gathered speed, my hands were still tied behind my back, my whole body hurt with discomfort and I knew I was still haemorrhaging from the birth.

"What have they done to Tommy?"

But I knew what they had done, wrapped him up in a piece of hessian sacking and put him in the biscuit tin, covered in brown paper like a package tied with thick twine and lowered into the ground. This is the one secret that will haunt me day and night. I tried to reach down and drag him out of the pit but a hand restrained me and I looked at the horror-struck faces around me.

I cried silently. There was no one to listen.

The car drove on through the cold January evening, away from home, away from Tommy, and we began the long journey across the Yorkshire landscape with bare, frostbitten hedgerows passing at great speed.   In front of my eyes there was the flicking of the windscreen wipers on the misted-up windows. Later, I don't know how much later, the road started to rise and for the first couple of hundred yards the slope was so extreme and the roads became narrow and twisted. We came to a crossroads and took the top of two roads and as the car crawled higher still and brought the sea into view at a distance and across the bay there were dark-green stretches with vague industrial shapes which were beginning to mist over in the background. The road continued onwards and upwards overlooking the sides of a deep valley.

I was beginning to see the awful power of fate, its deviousness, the way it could wipe out in an instant the things I had been certain I could rely on, my home, my little sister Rosie, Nana and Michael. He would marry some other girl. Someone else would walk with him through the purple heather and down to our stream where as children we had sailed our paper boats. She would be the one to hold his hand, to help with the baby lambs, to run laughing through the lashing rain to the nearest hut.

It was now a pitch-black night, with nothing to look at but the road ahead, lit by the occasional headlights of another car. The land rolled and dipped, climbing higher and deeper into the mountains towards "The Manor". My prison! But they called it an asylum. What was an asylum? A sanctuary? A safe haven?"

"We're here," the driver said with a sigh of relief and there it stood in front of us. The darkness crept down, the rain drummed on the steel roof of the van and we got out. There was a roaring in my ears, the pulse at my temples was hammering painfully, my eyes were staring from their sockets and my arms and legs felt numb. The building was dark. The long black shape in the greater darkness of trees and sky made me think of death, its tall chimneys silhouetted against the dark sky.

The moon appeared from behind the black clouds shining on so many windows. That was my first impression, a hulk of a building crammed with windows, vast windows downstairs, and windows crammed together on the upper floors and rows of small windows reaching right up to the top of the gables and into the roof. The car pulled into a wide courtyard at the front, the driver stopped at a large entrance door and somebody turned a key in the lock. At that instant my mind came into focus and I felt a shiver down my spine at the enormous granite strength and stillness of the building. "The Manor". My new home.

The wind whipped through my body as I was led out of the van and passed into a life of total helplessness, facing the vast grey future.

They flung open the front door into a large entrance hall which would swallow up our tiny farm house.. The heavy door with its many locks and bolts clanked shut and when it closed behind me, I heard the key grind in the lock.

I was destined to be lonely forever. Fr. Lynch had seen to that, and Uncle Johnny, I thought.
Even now I could smell him. The reek of stale sweat and tobacco seemed to hang in the air. His presence was so tangible that I almost expected him to appear. He was always there in my nightmares. I watched him advance as if in slow motion.

Then I was inside those solid walls that now stood between me and freedom. The floor began to tilt. A nurse guided me as I took my first faltering steps into my new world. This particular form of other life started to unnerve me. I felt like being a prisoner on death row, who must survive day after day and become accustomed to this life. Ahead of me was an eternity of emptiness.

"Follow me," Matron said.

They led me into a cold, cheerless room. A warden and a young woman in a white coat sat behind a desk. A second lady in white, and Matron in her navy, neatly-pressed uniform went over and sat next to them. I was left standing in front of a large oak desk. There were some sheaves of paper, a decanter of water and glasses.

They sentenced me on the strength of a doctor who had never seen me, on a decision made by Fr. Lynch who had all the authority to speak. The atmosphere was so inhibiting but there was a little relief when they eventually removed the handcuffs. My head started to spin and I reached out. Someone, who noticed that I was holding onto the side of the desk for support, offered me a chair.

For the rest of my life I would think of Nana. I would see her that moment, reaching out to catch me before I fell. I saw her again waving over her shoulder, her grey hair falling over one eye as she was brutally pushed indoors. I wanted to hold her, to touch her.

Matron was the first to speak. "This letter from Fr. Lynch gives me all the details but I need to fill out some more forms. Can you please confirm your name is Kathy Lavelle?"

I nodded.

"Today's date, 8th January 1952." She looked up.

I just stood there in a daze. It was almost midnight and I was collapsing with exhaustion.

"Your date of birth, 9th September 1936?" she said in a louder voice. I nodded again.

"Another New Year," she smiled around at everyone, "and I hope it's a good one for all of us."

"Age 16?"
"Yes," I whispered.

She checked my home address and the other details on Fr. Lynch's letter, such as our doctor's name, family solicitor and the school's headmaster. Later I was to realise that none of these people were aware of what was happening. They trusted Fr. Lynch. The whole village had placed him on a pedestal and now he had taken full responsibility for my fate.

My mind was in a blur. Then one of the ladies, who wore a nurse's watch, came over to me. She took out an inch tape and measured me for the standard green asylum smock but I just wanted to curl up in a warm bed with Nana's arms wrapped around me and Rosie breathing silently on the other side. The warden in shirtsleeves sat there staring at me and saying nothing. A tray of drinks arrived and eventually someone gave me a cup of tea.

"Here love. A hot drink is what you need." She was Shirley, the cook supervisor. I was to get to know her much later. In fact she was to become one of my allies and liberators. But now I just welcomed a friendly face and these were the first kind words that had been spoken to me since my arrival.

"Just one more thing. We need to take a photo. It is procedure to take an 'arrival' photo and then another on the day you leave." I felt the air go out of my lungs and I slumped in the chair. Then I pulled myself up and tried my best to look at the camera. "No, you don't need to smile. Just a normal expression!"

"What was normal?" I wondered. I found out later that they wanted me to look as miserable and as mental as possible.

"Now, sign this." The Matron placed a wad of papers at the front of the desk. I stared down at a whole lot of legal jargon that I didn't really understand but I signed through my tears.

"You are no longer a prisoner," Matron said. "You are a patient now." My identity was changed from a murderess and a person of vilest hatred to something broken that must be mended. I was now an object of concern and care. I was to be analysed, given various medications, cured and eventually released, but when would that day come?

Grief gnawed into my soul. I was tortured by the memory of all the simple things I had lost, the little farm house, a ride on the hay float, paddling in the stream with Michael, pushing Rosie on the old swing on the apple tree and Nana's warm arms holding me. I watched it all slip away from me. My future was to be in this large, echoing house on the moors and I was panicking like the mad woman they said I was.

Kathy Lavelle

Chapter 3

Then I was taken to my room.

"Follow me!" A firm hand led me by the arm. I couldn't tell if it was man or woman with short cropped hair and oversized uniform. The size, shape and bearing were nondescript. I was guided through the dark entrance into a large hall. Several steps led up to the first floor by a broad stairwell, but the stairs became narrower above, curving steeply upwards.

Every step was an effort. When I was faced with stairs my legs could scarcely carry me. As we climbed higher, I noticed it got colder, a coldness which dominated the whole hulk of the building. Doors slammed shut and bolts slid into place as we went from one area to another. We continued along more corridors, through another security door and then into a long dimly-lit hallway and finally up a very narrow flight of stairs into the small room.

It was a dreary little room with a table, a wooden chair and a cracked mirror on the wall. The room was cold and I shivered violently. The bedroom window looked out on the cold night and the dark shrouded buildings below. The silence and the austerity had an oppressive quality. There was no heating in those days. The bed was covered with grey army blankets, a strange bedroom, like a little prison cell, in a strange building and all my courage had trickled away.

There was a murmured, "Good night!" The door was bolted and the heavy footsteps retreated back down the stairs.

After the door slammed shut and the bolt slid into place, I was alienated, lost and abandoned. It seemed to me that the building had swallowed me whole, wrapped around me and squashed me to death, smothering and suffocating my mind and body

"Maybe they are right," I thought. "Maybe I am mad." My thoughts went back to when I held my sister Rosie close in our little warm bed or cuddled in with Nana when Rosie had spread herself out taking up all the space.

I sat on the side of the bed, rocking and staring out at nothing. Then I remembered Nana's words. Despite my exhaustion, I undid the tacking thread from the hem of my dress and found the small gold ring and the note.

"This is my wedding ring, the only thing I can give you. Keep it safe and remember I am with you no matter what. You'll be back one day. Keep telling yourself that." This was my only treasure from the only one in the world who loved me and now we were worlds apart, never to see each other again. There was also a crinkled photo of Nana. I pressed it to my lips.

I pulled the thin army blankets over my head. Nowadays people tell me that places for the sick and mad are bright and attractive, a sort of cheerfulness to alleviate people's miseries, but this place had an institutional grimness.

"This building is a death-trap," Shirley told me later, "It has been scandalously neglected and never properly funded."

My whole world had been contracted into this small room but my mind still roamed freely across the ploughed fields with Michael. I loved him. We were the same age and I think he loved me too but we were now in different worlds, poles apart. Everywhere was hushed and cold. Not an item of life anywhere. I was trapped, swallowed up by the moors with nothing but the whitewashed wall glaring back at me.

I curled up beneath the thin blankets, but time had stopped and everything was crowding in on me. The spy hole opened at twenty-minute intervals through the night, or so I was told later, but apart from that I was left alone in a nocturnal world teeming with evil spirits. Shirley told me later that I had been on suicide watch.

As I lay there listening to outside noises, one of my few vivid recollections of early childhood had to do with a winter evening when I was about four or five years old. I remembered the warm kitchen and the hot fire, the wonderful feeling of being wanted from quite an early age and how good it felt to be washed in front of the fire. Uncle Johnny always got a towel and dried me on his knee. Then we all sat together round the small table for supper in front of the roaring peat fire. But I know now that Johnny was grooming me.

The Baby In The Biscuit Tin

In my mind I was running, running from Johnny and then in my haste I tripped over stones and almost went sprawling. I ran the last bit towards the house. As the door closed behind me I felt my legs give way. I had no courage, no spirit. I could feel the tears coming, nerves and fury mixed together. How ugly I had become in their eyes, how wicked, and I felt ashamed, my self esteem torn to shreds. That life as I'd know it was gone forever.

I cried myself to sleep every night. The asylum's merciless control was simply a form of imprisonment, mistaking sanity for madness. They led me through the doorway into a world of great terror and I glimpsed the shadowy barrier between the past and the present, and knew keenly the physical ache of being unable ever to go back.

Chapter 4

My death sentence came in 1952. I had been buried alive, simply disappeared as so many had done before me, leaving not a trace in the outside world. I thought of Tommy back there, which seemed like a thousand miles away, lying beneath cruel snow and this would cause me a thousand sleepless nights. All hopes and dreams had crumbled around me. I must have dozed off eventually but bells started to ring throughout the building and the church clock struck seven.

Someone moaned down the next corridor. It was even darker and colder. Immediately I started listening to the noises. A board had creaked on the floor below and a moment later there were more moans and distant screams echoing through the building. Later, I don't know how much later, I heard slow, heavy, regular footsteps coming up the stairs.

"Follow me," a person said. She was Helen, who had been assigned to keep watch over me for the first few days.

I was taken down into a huge area divided up into lots of different sections, there were tables, chairs, sofas, a piano and large windows through which I could see the grey sky and low clouds. At the far end was the refectory and I was guided to a table in a quiet corner quite a distance from the other patients. Helen hovered in the background. A final gong sounded for breakfast and hand-in-hand huge numbers of patients trooped into the dining room like school children, old people shuffled in on two sticks and a girl not much older than myself was pushed through the door in a wheelchair.

"I will put you sitting with Angel," Helen whispered. "Be sure you try and get her to eat something."

I started speaking in low tones, and my eyes were fixed on the ground but someone jumped up and slapped me on the face. It was as though I awakened suddenly to what was going on around me. It was only Angel and it was some sort of gesture of friendship.

In the main refectory area I could hear the tantrums. Old people gossiped, or cried and giggled like babies. Others stared into space like zombies. The place was full of mad people and lots of big red faced women talking and gesticulating loudly. The arguing and laughing and singing and shouting echoed through the wide spaces. Suddenly someone screeched like a wounded animal. I had never heard such a horrible sound.

"It's always like this," Shirley came and placed a large bowl of porridge on the table. I remembered her from the night before, the only person who had shown a glimmer of kindness. She laid a gentle hand on my shoulder.

"You will get used to it," she said.   Then she bent and whispered in my ear. "Try and get Angel to eat something." But we both sat there staring at the food. The supervisors were too busy trying to calm people down. I had already started to find it hard to distinguish between dreams, reality and memory and a surge of rage rushed though me

When I closed my eyes everything around me just felt empty and cold as if I was in the loneliest place in the world, in the middle of nowhere. I could hear the sound of my own heartbeat and the wind in the trees. I just sat there and gradually found myself dozing off to sleep from the exhaustion of the day before.

Suddenly memory took flight. The power of moving through space and time allowed me to sit there with Nana. I played with her dress and she fondled my hair. I stroked the long delicate fingers on her calloused hands. Then I was with Michael. Hand in hand we walked home along the stream. They had locked me up forever but no one could prevent these exquisitely happy journeys when I floated back in time.

Michael and I were walking through the heather on the hillside. I felt the sun on my head, and the breeze from the snow on the hilltops cool on my back. Our fingers locked together. Below us the curl of the falling water and the spray from the dam were blowing in the wind. I was back by our stream watching the clear water flowing between the rocks. The silver waters lapped softly at our feet. Everything was happiness and singing when I was a young girl. We did not have electricity or running water or sadness either. Not yet. In my dream I watched that tyre swinging back and forth, back and forth pushing Rosie higher and higher into the apple blossoms.

The wild flowers, the murmur of streams, the taste of plums that our garden gave us in such abundance, and the smell of the wild roses, all this ran before my eyes. It was a talking picture, one in which I hear Nana's voice, always affectionate and kind and the barking of Carlow the sheep-dog calling me into the garden to play.

Such sweet gentle memories and emotions! I could smell the land and this gave me such pleasure. In my fit of nostalgia, I was back there with Michael, sitting on the river bank, the leaves swaying gently in the water.

"Will you marry me," he asked. "I mean when we are old enough and when we have asked our parents." I just laughed, not knowing if he was serious. Sitting on the edge of the hillside, I could still feel the tangible weight of a baby lamb in my arms and the warmth of its fleece. I felt a peace fall over me. Michael protected me. We liked to put our hands in the stream and feel the water rush through our fingers.

But it wasn't Michael. I awoke with a start. It was Helen, my career. She tapped me on the shoulder. "Everyone's gone," she said as she started clearing the tables. "You haven't eaten a thing and no doubt Angel has escaped again." She poured me a glass of milk and sat with me until I had finished.

"They are all out in the exercise yard", she said and led me back through the refectory and towards the lounge. There were a dozen or so battered old chairs leaning against the walls and a large radiogram in the corner. She pulled an old cloak from a peg inside the door and wrapped it around my shoulders before I was led out into the cold courtyard. I stood there looking from one distorted face to another listening to their babble of enraged squabbles.

This gave vent to all my own hurt and anger. Mine was a tale of horror. I had been removed from my own home to a house in a desolate area and I was introduced to strange people, mad people whom I wouldn't ordinarily meet. What does anyone know of me anyway? Old people shuffle along and smile with sunken eyes and mumble and dribble their food and no one sees a frightened sixteen-year-old. "Had I become one of them?" I wondered.
But I was too young to be one of them and I needed my baby but I knew that I could never have Tommy back.

Kathy Lavelle

Chapter 5

It was my second night alone, or maybe my third or fourth. Maybe it was months later, but it was not any better than the first. I watched the fresh snow flakes rushing up out of the darkness past the window. A cold terror lay in the pit of my stomach along with the hunger. I had never been so terrified, so alone. The sense of loss was so painful, I began to block out the memories and tried hard to drive those fears from my mind but some memories are not so easy to push away. In the mirror I was white-faced and trembling.

I have a head full of stories about the past. But I don't think my story is like that of other people.

I clearly remember one particular evening coming up to my fifteenth birthday. Nana and I were alone that evening. The others had gone down to the village to get cattle food and groceries. In the early twilight, an old gipsy woman, wrapped in a black shawl knocked at the door and then came into the house.

"Cross my hand with silver," she said and Nana searched down to the bottom of her apron pocket to find a new sixpence.

She read my palm in the light of the blazing fire and made her gloomy predictions.

"Your life will be filled with many hardships," she said.

"What kind of hardships?" I asked.

"Ah, you must wait and see but I warn you to be very careful out there on those lonely moors." I shuddered and suddenly the room went cold. Nana went and laid some fresh peat on the fire and gave it a gentle poke to fan the flames. Then it was her turn for the hand-reading. The old gypsy demanded another sixpence so Nana put her hand back in her apron pocket and gave up her last coin.

"And you. Beware of losing your treasures. Don't trust anyone."

When she had gone Nana said, "She's only a silly old woman. She can't have the powers to foresee the future. It's all just a bit of fun. Pay no heed to what she says and don't worry yourself about anything. There are no dangers around here and there is no one I would distrust in this neighbourhood." I thought no more about it but in my tiny room, it all came flooding back.

My mind wandered back to another evening, not long after the gypsy's visit, when I was sent on an errand to Auntie Jean's across the hillside. She was Uncle Johnny's wife, a nervous woman but she was always kind and gentle with me and often gave me something to take back home, usually a cake she had baked herself.

On the way back the full force of the wind caught me. My eyes and my brain were now filled with the vision of a man. I could see Johnny, his long black coat flapping in the rain. He strode towards me with his hands in his pockets. I glanced anxiously round and suddenly I had a sort of inner fear and could feel the chillness of the water bedside me. He waved his stick and yelled curses at me.

I looked past him into the gloom. He was now so close I could see the dark stubble on his face. The river was overflowing its banks again. I kept walking but he was blocking my way. He came nearer, put his face so close to mine that I could smell him. I was too afraid to yell out, too frightened to leave and powerless to resist. He was much stronger than I was, heavily muscled and powerful, a big man. My uncle. Here was a man who should have been looking out for me, protecting me. He was my father's only brother and they did everything together on the farm. No one would ever believe my story. I trembled with terror as he grabbed me and, pushing me to the ground, forced me to submit to his tyrannical will. My fear increased and a shudder passed through my body, like the fear of death or like death itself.

Suddenly I could hardly breathe, and he was speaking in that fierce harsh voice threatening me. He gave his unpleasant laugh and in a frenzy he left abruptly with the words. "If you tell anybody, you're dead. Do you hear me? Dead!" he yelled after me, "and you'll rot in hell."

If I had known the things that he would do to me, it would have been much better to have killed myself first. I got up and stumbled away blindly into the freezing night, dreading the long walk home. In my mind's eye, I still see him walking away from me down the hillside. I'd watched as my uncle walked away through the cattle grid and round the corner and then I turned and looked up at the rock face above me glowing red in the sunset, bright red like blood.

Afterwards it was all chaos and confusion. I was toppling over the rocks, a hand flung out wildly in front as if to steady myself. The wind was strengthening steadily and the river rising. At the edge of the river the waterfall cascaded down the high banks of the large stream with swift currents towards the small tributary and the combined watercourses bubbled over the rocks.

"Why not just fling myself over the weir and end this torment?" I thought as I lay in a bruised heap in the mud near the water, too tired, too weak, and too miserable to move.

A wave of pain engulfed me with every step and blood began to ooze down my swollen leg. Spots swam before my eyes, my head whirled, everything went dark and I slumped to the ground. I picked myself up, tears welled up and streamed down my face as I pushed aside branches, and crawled over moss-covered logs. Glancing back over my shoulder all the while, I caught my breath as a swift blur of movement, a monstrous wild cat vaulted high over a towering rock. I stopped in my track, stark terror charging through my body. Then I fled in a wild panic. In my panic it was only instinct that led me to the small farm house. My side was aching and I was gasping for breath.

Fortunately for me, my parents were out in the byre milking the cows and Rosie was playing in the bedroom.

"My god child, what has happened?" Nana asked. She took me in her arms and I burst into tears, breaking into convulsions of sobs.

"Shh!" she said. "Come and I'll clean you up and get you some dry clothes."

I could see myself in the mirror over the mantelpiece and could not believe that the dreadful sight I saw was really me, my hair in disarray and it looked like I hadn't been washed for months. It was some time before Nana got the whole story. She had guessed some of it but was totally shocked when she heard that the abuser was Uncle Johnny. I will never forget how Nana had supported me in the months ahead.

And here now in "The Manor" was my indeterminate future, my home, and the idea of absolute insanity which we all associate with the very name of an asylum. My life was in turmoil. I was rejected, exiled from the real world in which people lived and worked and loved. It was as if I were condemned to live the rest of my life incarcerated within these high walls. They had thrown me like a criminal into this empty lifeless place. I wondered about the journey of my life which had taken me from so much hope to such despair. Then it stopped. I tried to calm myself, induce myself into feeling relieved but my whole world had lain in shattered fragments around me when my mind could no longer function.

Later Meg was to tell me that many people at some point in their life feel darkness around them. But that was before I met Meg and I was alone in my misery.

Chapter 6

It was a painful day the first time I met Doctor Mac.

A few weeks after I arrived at "The Manor", I was lost somewhere deep inside myself where I couldn't reach and no one else could, not ever Shirley. I was still a young girl and still needed to be wanted, to be cuddled, by Nana. The only time I could cuddle Tommy was when I had a happy dream and held my baby in my arms. Shirley had tried to stop me feeling sorry for myself and I tried my best to think of others before myself but memories of Johnny and Dad wouldn't go away. Johnny had used and abused me and dad was always quick to slap us down if we set a foot wrong. I was scared of him whenever I made the slightest mistake.

Then came the big recriminations when he found out I was pregnant. He became more violent and unpredictable and I never knew what was going to happen. The relationship was turbulent and Nana was afraid to intervene. They had conspired against me, my Dad, Uncle Johnny and Fr. Lynch.

"It's time for your appointment," Nurse Frances said as she came to fetch me. She led me into the doctor's surgery. I almost reeled over with the shock. This was the first time I had direct contact with a man since my incarceration.

 Doctor Mac looked so much like my Dad, a fleshy man with grey curly hair, broad shoulders and a high colour. He was even dressed in Dad's Sunday jacket. When I saw the shape, I could feel the blood draining out of my face. He nodded solemnly, more to himself than to me, looking out onto the side garden.

Doctor Mac was sitting behind a large oak desk, reading a newspaper. The paper was spread out on his desk and he had that same smug expression on his face which Dad used when he read the Sunday newspapers. There was the sound of rustling papers as he peered over the top of his glasses and opened the file of Father Lynch's brief notes in front of him, with the incriminating story of my life, my life written on a few sheets of manuscript.

"Did you harm your baby? he asked without welcoming me or introducing himself. "I have it here before me but you know we are here to help you. That's why you are not in a secure prison. You were transferred here on the grounds of diminished responsibility."

I knew that he was making a truly horrifying accusation against me. When he asked if I had harmed my baby, I knew he was talking about murder and this was why I was condemned here to a life of reparation for my sins.

"Did you harm your baby?" he asked again.

"No, I didn't," my voice was scarcely audible.

"I need to discover if you are suffering from paranoia," he said. "Some things must be covered up and buried so the shame of them doesn't taint the next generation," he said.

I didn't know what shame he was talking about. I could feel his eyes staring vacantly and the agitation growing in him. Behind the horn-rimmed glasses, his eyes were black and watchful. Distrustful. I could feel those eyes on me but I didn't look up. He tried to get me talking but I clammed up.

Then he pushed his head forward, and looking up over the top of his glasses at me he asked again, "Did you harm your baby?"

"No," I said. My voice was almost a whisper.

Doctor Mac was just going through the motions. He wasn't paying very much attention to anything. He sat in his tall swivel chair and said nothing more for a while. The small light from the window illuminated his dark, intimidating face. Then he picked up his pen and scratched something across the paper.

"I have hundreds of other patients to attend, to see if they can be placed back in the community. Some may be released and others," he paused, "I'm afraid will remain here. But they will get help, and medication and lots of physical work to keep their minds occupied. We try to do as much as we can in the way of justice depending on the seriousness of the allegations made against them. But you have nothing to fear, we will give you all the help you need. Have any of your relatives visited you yet?"

I told him they hadn't and I spoke as quietly and calmly as I could but I was becoming dizzy.

"I think that's best. You know that when patients have visitors, it always upsets them and we are right back where we started in their programme of treatment." He leaned back on his chair and took a sip from a glass.

I knew now that if anyone did want to come, they would be denied visiting rights. Anyhow Nana was too old and frail for the journey even if anyone agreed to travel with her and Rosie was too young. I didn't want either of them to see this place. The full magnitude of my situation had now crashed down upon me. I was to be buried here for the rest of my life and never see my family again. Dr. Mac would see to that.

He said, "Try and look on the bright side of life," but his words, "Did you harm your child?" were ringing in my ears. When he then asked me if I had settled in, I tried to stammer a reply but fell silent. Every time I had to give an answer my voice sounded small and thin. Then I collapsed.

"You'll be fine. You passed out for a moment that's all." Nurse Frances spoke calmly. I had been coming in and out of consciousness, trying to steady myself and could feel tears spring up behind my eyes but I was determined that I wouldn't allow them to appear.

The nurse put a thermometer in my mouth and waited. She shook the mercury down.
"You are all right. The colour is beginning to come back in your cheeks." She handed me a glass of water. The cool water revived me and I was now ready to leave.

Doctor Mac went on speaking as if nothing had happened. "I just wanted to uncover the facts," he said.

He took up his pen and scratched something else on the paper. Then he picked up the
prescription pad.

"I am putting you on a high dose of antidepressants," he said.

The whole interview made me nervous and he rose, not to shake my hand as I left, but to fill his glass from the jug on the sideboard. Shirley told me afterwards that she thought his water was laced with gin. He rose like an all-seeing giant, towering above me and he didn't even glance in my direction as Nurse Frances led me out of the room. Shirley came to the rescue with a hot drink and a slice of cake. "There's plenty I can tell you about Dr. Mac," she said "but not now. You just sit down and relax. Over here love,"

After I started taking the antidepressants, I began to suffer the side effects. I found I was gaining a lot more weight. They made me feel thirsty and most of the time I felt disorientated and afraid.

One morning Shirley said "There's only one place for that lot." She grabbed them and threw them in the bin.

Chapter 7

It was strange how I hadn't noticed Meg before. I had been there for about six weeks and on that particular morning I sat in the refectory staring into my breakfast, thinking about Nana and baby Tommy and my little sister Rosie. I think Meg noticed the tears in my eyes.

At first I thought Meg was a member of staff but I soon found out she was one of us. The first time I saw her, she wore a pale blue shift dress with a pattern of little white flowers, so different from our dreary green uniforms.

She didn't need to buy expensive clothes to look good. She had a kind face, a clear complexion and her hair was white, fine and soft as silk, and fastened with a clip at the back of her head. Her eyes were a beautiful sparkling blue and they crinkled around the sides when she smiled. It was clear she had always taken care of herself personally and she was meticulously clean. Meg was a small slight woman of about forty years who would eventually give me the gift of hope although I didn't know that yet. Most of all I noticed her bearing and composure, she moved with a grace that seemed to come from some great inner wisdom.

After breakfast, she laid a gentle hand on my shoulder and led me to her small bedroom at the back of the kitchen. I found myself drawn to her and she was to become the silver lining where there were so many dark clouds.

"What will happen to us?" I asked.

"Don't worry," she smiled and put her arms around me. This friendship of ours had been forged early. There was something quite different about Meg. Her character was captured in her face. Kindness and serenity radiated from her eyes.

"Every trial endured makes a soul nobler and stronger than it was before," she said.

"You can be lured into self-destruction," she went on. "If you embrace despair, you sin against hope." I felt my heart thudding in my chest at these strange words.

"It just seems that we are bound to accept our fate," I said. "Dr. Mac has only driven me deeper into despair."

"Forget Dr. Mac," she said offering me a biscuit.

We looked out the small window into the exercise yard at the rows of silent people walking back and forth, back and forth. "You don't want to end up like these poor people," she said. "You must try to fit in with the other residents. You don't want them to think you're crazy. Do you?"

"Everyone else does," I said.

"No of course not. Nobody thinks that. I certainly don't think you're crazy."

Meg helped me pull myself back from the wreckage of that day. She was the first person since Nana who had befriended me, to make me care enough. There was something about my desperation that made her feel sorry for me and she helped me to help myself.

"Listen to me......" she paused, "Life is a journey. You don't need power or wealth to survive but with love in your heart you can face every snowstorm."

"But my life is turned upside down. What am I to do?" I sat there trying to make sense of her words. "Does the pain ever go away?"

"Not really but at some point life starts up again and the pain becomes easier to bear. "I'm here for you, but you must try to help yourself," she told me. "Look at yourself, your lovely eyes and your beautiful blonde hair. You radiate a halo of beauty and good looks. Believe in yourself. Take pride in your appearance."

There were to be many sessions like this with Meg and I always returned to my room with renewed vitality. I began to build up my self-esteem. I looked in the mirror. It was true I had soft hair like gold and my eyes were the brightest blue like Nana's.

"No one can pull anyone back from anywhere. You must save yourself," she had told me over and over again. Later she said, "No one is in charge of your happiness but you. Time heals almost everything. Give it time," she held my hand and gently led me through the gardens that led down to the farm.

"I don't think it will ever heal," I told her.

"However good or bad a situation is it will change. Believe me," she tried her best to reassure me. "There is no cloud so black that a glimmer of sun doesn't shine through."

"But I can't stand the nothingness."

I looked across at the farmyard and saw the line of cattle being led out of the milking sheds, and across the fields to the pasture. The tractor was setting off to another side of the farm and I could see a crowd of young people riding on the trailer laughing and nudging each other.

"I would like to work on the farm," I said. "It would remind me of home".

"Oh no, you don't want to work on the farm. Believe me. I have seen the girls come in with chilblains, headaches, crying from pain in their backs. Frank, the foreman is a tyrant. Worse still, he has no understanding of the needs of young girls, or young men either for that matter. We older folk are lucky. We are exempt from all that manual labour. You would enjoy a little job in the kitchen. At least you'll be inside in the warmth and there's always a cup of tea on the ready. I'll ask Shirley if she can use another pair of hands."

Meg arranged it all. She was greatly respected by the other patients. She also had the respect of all the staff. She had authority and was asked for advice if there were problems, and if she intervened in an argument her decision was accepted and respected. It was all arranged. I was to start my duties in the kitchen the following day.

The next morning I rose at dawn and quickly got washed and dressed. "Shirley is a bit of a rough diamond, but her heart is in the right place" Meg told me and then she took me down and formally introduced me. The kitchen was huge, with copper pots and kettles hanging in rows on the stone walls. "Four hundred inmates to be fed four times a day," Meg waved her hands across the vastness.

Shirley was a plump, pleasant lady, always happy, always singing. She and her helpers were in white cotton aprons neatly washed and ironed on a daily basis.

"You Are My Sunshine" was playing on the wireless and Shirley sang along as she waltzed over and gave me a great big hug.

31

"Come in Kathy," she said. "I hope you'll be happy here". She was already lighting the gas under the copper for tea, slicing and buttering a chunk from the fresh loaf. Pots were already bubbling on the enormous cookers. "A cuppa tea love before I show you the ropes."

I had a feeling of nostalgia; it was almost like the way that Nana had looked after all of us, singing while she worked. I wanted to tell Shirley that she was the first friendly face I had met the night I arrived but I was still too shy. But I know I did tell her many times over in the months and years ahead. The kitchen was warm, the gas hissing quietly below large pots.
There was a small table with a few chairs in one corner and Shirley insisted that I sit down and have my tea first. Then she sent me into her office to find a hair band. Her desk was orderly, pens and order forms in place and trays of papers at the ready.

She tore a leaf from the calendar and smoothing down her apron, she began teaching me my duties."I want you to take it easy for the first few days," she said.

"It's okay," I said. "I need to keep busy."

Shirley lifted down the large iron frying pans and placed them on the cookers. The bacon was sizzling nicely on racks inside the ovens and I was looking all around the kitchen, taking in all the new and wonderful sights. There were two enormous refrigerators inside the back door and a walk-in cold room for all the perishables. Close to the pantry was a small storeroom where they kept the sacks of flour and hung the cured meats. There were three other girls in the kitchen and I soon found out that Shirley was a kind and caring person. I began work at one task or another, washing up, scraping carrots and slicing potatoes.

No matter how difficult the tasks or how unpleasant, in the kitchen Shirley always made sure there was music and laughter. The kitchen was one of the largest rooms in the building and contained the massive stoves, the biggest sink I had ever seen, a tub, a boiler and various dressers and kitchen cabinets Shirley was taller than I was and super-fit with dark brown, short-cropped hair, hazel green eyes and a ready smile in spite of all that had happened to her. Later I found out that Shirley was a patient like the rest of us and she had her own sad story.

"Everyone here has a story to tell," Meg had told me.

I spent my mornings here, and learned how to take pride in my work. The kitchen was clean and bright with its tall windows and large, scrubbed work surfaces. Shirley even taught me how to scrub the wooden table. "With the grain," she said, "back and forth, back and forth getting out the last morsel of dirt and then rinsing with clean cold water."

Then it was lunch time. After all the preparation and the setting of tables, the arrival of so many hungry bodies soon amplified the sounds in the dining room. This became the noisiest place on earth, with people pushing and shoving to get closest to the serving hatches. Wardens had to stand policing the queues and this was when fights often broke out and people were moved to the back of the line for bad behaviour, like naughty schoolchildren. Lunch was a rowdy time but now I was privileged to eat in the kitchen in a more civilised way. We sat around the small table after everyone else had been served and the place became blissfully quiet when most patients had moved out into the exercise yards or back to the dormitories.

Wherever there was work to be done, I liked to keep my hands busy. I was safely installed in the kitchen and that is where I stayed until the next chapter of my life. In the beginning I was exhausted after a hectic morning's work but the afternoon was free time.

"What am I supposed to do with all this spare time?" I asked Meg.

"You will soon find a great deal to do. After being up at five o'clock and working solidly until lunch is served, the first thing you must do is take a rest," Meg was right. This was when I began to sleep more soundly, sometimes right through the afternoon and then through the night as well, mainly from exhaustion.

Kathy Lavelle

Chapter 8

Meg had been my best friend in the house for as long as I could remember. "When you're busy you don't think of what should have been," she used to say. She made me feel I had found a sort of family. Our day was divided into sections by bells. We ate, slept, worked and exercised by bells.

"You wouldn't have wanted to work on the farm," Meg reminded me. "Patients who work in the fields might be some distance from the main buildings. Some patients don't want to work outdoors particularly those who come from the city. They find gardening or agricultural work degrading, preferring to work indoor as cleaners and at less arduous jobs. Some work as assistants to tailors, upholsterers, carpenters and blacksmiths or have taken up knitting and embroidery classes. Supervisions in workshop have to be strict disciplinarians. Heavy tools could be lethal or used as weapons for self-harm."

Meg was everyone's favourite. She was gentle, soft-spoken and always comforted anyone who needed to be reassured.

But Shirley was different. She talked and talked as she worked. "This place is full of perverts, alcoholics and all sorts of abusers. And the people who treat them are sometimes worse. I've seen them all - psychiatrists, neurologists, psychotherapists, nutritionists, psychologists and all the other 'ists' in the world. Some of the patients can't sleep, they can't eat, or they wash their hands too much. Everyone's got their own story. And you know something; monsters are let off on small technicalities every day."

One cold evening, Meg led me into her small room, offered me a chair, held her thin hands in mine, bent forward and kissed me on the forehead. Then she went through to her small kitchenette and put on the kettle. I sat with my hands in my lap, but what a cheerful, comforting sight the steaming kettle made. I was still very shy but I no longer felt alone.

"It's up to us to make this a haven, a sanctuary from the bitter world outside," she said. She was sitting on her bed, sunlight streaming through the open window and a gentle breeze blowing the flimsy curtains. There was a photo by her beside. It looked like a younger version of herself with a handsome man in Air Force uniform who had his arm around her. A very pretty little baby with white curly hair sat on her lap. Then I started thinking about her past. This was the first time I gave a thought to the plights of others. She was very pretty and seemed to be happily married, a very different story from my own. But why was she in a place like this? I had a vague sense that she had been transferred here from happier times like I had but that must have been many years before.

"Why is she here," I wondered again but didn't like to ask.

As I sat wrapped up in my own thoughts, Meg was chatting away about the lovely weather but then suddenly she broke off. She checked her hair, re-pinning it neatly with her fingers.
"You've had a tough time," she said. "I have been watching you and I can tell. You have a broken heart but you are not alone in that respect."

I was so affected by hearing another human speak to me with such grace and respect that I started to outpour my tragic story and those awful years of deepening depression and shock, and then the recriminations that I had endured.

I didn't know why I was telling her these things, except for her infectious personality or the fact that I was comfortable with her. She was easy to talk to and was an oasis in the dessert.

"And here we are where psychiatrists hand out fistfuls of pharmaceuticals like dolly mixtures, to calm our madness. When I first came here, I was bewildered by the psychiatric labels they put on our illnesses." Meg looked across at me.

"It's not fair," I said. "My situation is hopeless."

"Don't say that. Hopelessness crushes the soul. We must try our best to find some kind of spirituality in this violent, thoughtless world."

Meg saw me looking at the photo on her small dressing table.

"I suppose you are wondering about my story. We all have our own unique story to tell. Mine is very different from yours." She placed the photo in my hand. "I was very happily married to Richard...." She paused. "He joined the Air Force but on his last mission he didn't come back." There was a long pause. She just sat there looking at the photo, her eyes clouding over.

I wanted to say something but couldn't find the right words.

"I had to keep going for the sake of Anna, my baby."

"Where is she now?" I asked.

Meg just sat there deep in thought, tears now more visible in her eyes.

"Anna was two when she died of meningitis. It was her second birthday. That was the most dreadful time for me. They said I had gone mental. One night they found me screaming on top of her grave. Richard's body was never found but we had his name inscribed on Anna's little pink tombstone. Shortly after that I was brought here. But sad to say it was my brother-in-law who instigated the whole thing and had our local doctor confirm that I was mentally insane. That is one reason I never wanted to go back." A cloud of sadness and listlessness suddenly came over her lovely face. I felt I had driven her like a turbulent wind into the depths of her sad past.

"I'm so sorry," was all I could say. "Oh my god," I thought. "What have they done to us?"

The pain in Meg's expression was too profound to measure. The intensity of these memories forced her to abandon me for a moment. She went into the kitchenette to wash a few cups and saucers. When she came back out her eyes were red and swollen. Now I realised that my strong heroine was hiding her own heartbreak.

"I've tried to pull down the curtain on my pains and hide them ever since I got here but I am unable to wipe them out of existence completely. This is the first time I have broken down in years and you must forgive me."

"Life isn't fair," I said.

"No, Life isn't fair but it's still good. In both our cases, there were people who thought we had brought dishonour to our families but I know that we have done nothing wrong. Life is too short to waste time hating anyone. Cry with someone. It's more healing than crying alone and helps to preserve your dignity. Make peace with your past so it won't mess up the present." I just sat and looked at her, letting her words sink in.

She looked at me and started to speak again as if she could read my thoughts and could see into my soul. "It is good to find a purpose in life, especially in this enormous place, to find something to occupy your time and energy. I mean something other than washing dishes and scraping carrots. I would like to help you find your niche, something simple to begin with but something to occupy your mind and keep your thoughts from straying. Brooding over things can never help anyone." Meg told me about her love of reading and writing. She had been a schoolteacher outside. "If it hadn't been for my books I really would have gone insane," she said.

"But I have never learned to read or write," I told her.

"We'll have to do something about that," she laughed.

Chapter 9

The memory of what happened next is patchy. My work in the kitchen kept me occupied with less time for brooding but there were good days and bad days. I was cut off from family, from life itself.

I went to bed and was meant to sleep. Up in the belfry the bell tolled the hours summoning me to atone for my sins. The clock struck two but I dosed off again. I had been sleeping, from sheer exhaustion, for a long time, before I was awakened again by heels clicking along the corridor mingled with other heavy determined steps. I knew every single sound in the building.

"I love my work in the kitchen but there are times when I find it difficult to drag myself out of bed." I told Meg. "Sometimes I lie there. I cry for Nana and for Tommy my baby."

"Things will change. I promise you." Meg tried to reassure me like she had done so often before. And Meg was right. Those were still the days before Charles' arrival and my whole life would be turned around. But in the meantime I had to try and make the most of it by keeping busy and by listening to Meg's words of wisdom.

Not long after I arrived they moved me from my small room in the attic into one of the dormitories on the floor below. There were fifteen beds and it was a long, narrow room with a space down the centre just wide enough for two people to pass. Each patient had a small cupboard leaning against the slanted walls.

One morning I woke up with a start. It was five a.m. and I tried to block out the noises. Still exhausted, I dragged myself out of bed and the un-curtained windows showed the lights of morning. I just stood there watching the cranes and piers and warehouses along the waterfront. I had used up all my tears and after a while I took refuge and comfort by jumping back into bed and finding a little comfort under the blankets. One minute I was here inside the walls of this massive, sprawling building and suddenly my memory transported me back to the little farm house where I was born and onto the hillside. The present and past all seemed to join together in a sort of kaleidoscope of shapes and colours, of happiness and sadness. In my dreams there were always flashes of home.

One thing I knew was I couldn't go back. I had already forged a life inside. I thought of how I had been betrayed by Johnny. When I was a child he seemed to love me. He used to laugh when I kissed him and said his whiskers tickled me. But he laid a mark on me that will be with me till the end of time. I didn't realise then but he already had designs on my body. It haunts my mind always. Because of him, I would never see my family again. Johnny was admired by the entire neighbourhood for his art of storyteller. He had a large collection of ghost stories, myths and legends which he told around the fire on a winter's night. He taught me all the fairy tales and nursery rhymes and hearing the rooks in the sky I could almost imagine I was back there on the mountainside. But he had shaped my life. It was hard to believe that he and Dad and Fr. Lynch were destined to destroy me and the very existence of my baby.

I started with a fright. I looked up at the bright sky, it was much later than I expected. The large buildings of the west wing loomed in front of me with their battered doors and original cast iron drainpipes still in place since Victorian days. Footsteps echoed on the bare boards of the long corridor and there was a knock on the door. It was Meg coming to rescue me, my new friend and surrogate mother, reminding me of the importance of holding on to my job in the kitchen. In a panic I leapt out of bed.

"You don't want anyone else to take your place," Meg warned. She put an arm around my shoulder in a rare moment of intimacy before I rushed to the wash rooms and then down to the kitchen.

When I arrived in the kitchen, I apologised to Shirley. She felt it was her duty, in front of the other girls, to reprimand me. Although her words were strict, the tone was gentle which made me feel comfortable with her again. Afterwards she said, "I know you have never been late before but I have to treat everyone equally. Don't worry about it. I'm sure you had a good reason this morning."

Shirley and I were becoming soul mates. My failures could always be softened by her humour and I was always willing to go that extra mile for her.

"The first couple of years are the toughest. Then it gets easier," Shirley said.

"Oh my God," I thought. How am I to survive that long? But if I had patience, there were better things to come, and they did come but I will tell you about that later.

The Baby In The Biscuit Tin

This morning my duties were to start kneading and sifting and baking biscuits and cakes. This was one of my favourite jobs and I went about my chores happily listening to the wireless and Shirley singing along to the latest hits.

"Cheer up little one," Shirley said as she handed me a hot drink. "This is a place full of old people, strange old people and old doctors. People said the psychiatrists had even gone mad too having worked so long surrounded by madness. It's a charming thought isn't it? But you young ones, you are the pick of the bunch. They wouldn't send you here if you weren't." The girls laughed. Shirley always did her best to lift our spirits.

Matron didn't often come into the kitchen so when she suddenly stood there in the doorway everyone was on their best behaviour.

"Have a seat Matron," Shirley said. "Kathy can you fetch a cup of tea for Matron."

When I brought the tea, Shirley had already opened the cake tin.

"Actually it was you I wanted to see Kathy," Matron said. "Come sit down. Shirley you pass us another cup of tea please."

"Thank you," I mumbled, taken aback and wondering what matron could possibly want with me. I hoped inwardly that she was not planning to move me to another department.

"Well I won't hang about," Matron said. "It's good news. We have found you your own little room under the stairs next to Meg. It's no mansion but has a small window and all the essentials.

I worried about the other girls who had been in the kitchen long before I arrived, but I found out that they had a small dormitory just for themselves and they didn't want to be split up.
"So there will be no jealousy," Shirley told me later.

I thanked Matron and she stood up and walked around inspecting what was going on and praising everyone for their hard work.

"You look after us well Shirley and you have a great team," she said

After lunch Shirley said, "I think this calls for a toast," and she started opening a bottle as Meg and the girls were handing glasses around and reaching up for the cake tin.

"To Kathy's new home!" Everyone raised their glasses. This was another new beginning.

I was still helping in the kitchen and was moving in and out of the storeroom fetching the things Shirley needed. The store was stocked from floor to ceiling with tins of fish, meat, tomatoes, fruit, vegetables and puddings, packets of sugar, flour, rice, pasta, oatmeal and huge bottles of cooking oil. Cardboard fruit boxes were stacked with the latest crop of apples and pears. Huge nets of carrots and parsnips hung on enormous hooks on the wall and there were large bins of potatoes standing at the far end. I knew how to fetch and carry, obey simple instructions but was barely literate. My future here in the kitchen was pretty much predestined. I knew how to prepare vegetables for cooking, do the ironing and boil the linen. I had all the skills I needed to survive.

But still the winter darkness began to seep into my soul. It seemed to last forever. The days had scarcely any daylight to them. They were achingly long and I was still growing impatient with the separation from my loved ones. The house was constantly veiled in a thick, sinister mist.

In the afternoons I often visited Meg to help cheer myself up. I would visit her in the narrow room next to mine. I had very little general knowledge and her conversations were awe-inspiring. I liked to sit on the large cushion at her feet, and listen to her sophisticated talk. She spoke with such authority and there was endurance as of perpetual youth about her.

I sat there wondering why I was still lonely, rootless and unhappy and overwhelmed by a nostalgia for Nana and my family and Michael. I wondered what he was doing now and thought of the last time I saw him. I was content then and secure, part of a family who had treated me well. I was wrapped in the warmth of Nana's arms and she sang me a little lullaby until my eyes closed in sleep. I could not accept the painful thought that this gloomy life was my destiny. This only caused my sorrows to burst forth even more. I often dreamed about the last time I was dragged out the door and then my eyes filled with tears, and at that moment my whole world dissolved.

Reading my thoughts, Meg said, "You don't want to bathe in your grief. It can crash in and destroy you. If you look out the window you can see the tiniest hint of sunshine coming from behind a black cloud." We sat in silence and thought about what she had just said.

"You can be saved from it all through love and kindness, to find yourself again, to recover the self you had lost, " Meg said "and you can become a human being who is not looked upon with scorn or despised. Trust me, you will be respected and cherished and made to feel special again. Just be patient. You are the one who determines your value."

As I walked down the corridor towards the side door, I saw a young woman seated in a wheelchair at a round table with two other women and a younger girl who was spoon-feeding her. When I went closer I noticed that she was in a poor condition. One side of her face had collapsed and sunken by time. She was paralysed around the left side of her mouth and her left leg was swollen and seemed to be without muscle tone. Her speech was halting and slightly slurred with long silences between words.

"Come and meet Mary," one of the other ladies waved across to me. "She just arrived yesterday and we have been asked to keep an eye out for her."

"Hello Mary," I said. "Welcome to "The Manor".

When the ladies had finished feeding Mary, they cleared the table and looked across at me.
"We have to go now. Do you think you could take Mary for a walk down the corridor and out into the yard for some fresh air?"

"Yes, that's fine," I said, "If that's all right with Mary."
"We will be back in half an hour. Ok?"

This was the first time I had the opportunity to help another fellow patient, apart from the time I was asked to look after Angel and let her down by falling asleep at the table.

I went over to the pegs inside the door and got two cloaks, one for each of us, and a warm blanket for Mary. She tried to tell me something but the words didn't make any sense to me. In a way I was glad that when we started walking I wouldn't have to listen to what she was trying to say. I knew I was being selfish but on the other hand this was all too difficult for me. What if she wanted to go to the toilet? I knew I couldn't cope. And what a relief when her carers came back! They would soon see to all her needs.

"Thanks," one of the ladies said. "You're a gem."

"No I'm not a gem," I thought. "I'm mean and selfish and consumed with self-pity." I had a long way to go until I was even a fraction like Meg. Her losses were as great as mine and yet she went around being nice to others instead of wallowing in her own grief.

Chapter 10

I had been there for two years when I met Meg one afternoon walking down the garden path. She came towards me.

"Come and I will show you something exciting." She took me by the hand and led me down a flight of steps behind the main entrance. Taking a key from her pocket, she opened the door of a dark and dusty room. These buildings had numerous small rooms tucked away   in all sorts of nooks and crannies and this one had a few broken shelves and dusty books scattered around.

"It used to be a library many years ago but there was such lack of interest, it became run down and then completely forgotten. I have my own stock of books in my room and I haven't been here for years," Meg told me.

I just looked around. The room seemed more a storage area than a library or a place where people could sit and read.   There were cobwebs on the windows, water gurgled through the pipes and there was debris scattered everywhere, old boxes, posters, picture frames and bits of broken furniture.

Meg looked around and a smile came over her face. "I think we could make something of this place."

Meg had never lost her enthusiasm and was always intent on making things better. She had begun to make me feel better too and now she wanted to improve this old shabby room. What I didn't realise then was that her aim was to improve my mind. I watched with interest over the next few days as Meg coerced a team of cleaners and soon most of the debris had been removed, light poured through the small window-panes with their tinted glass, amber and blood-red reflecting the spring sunshine. We started to take pride in developing our library, making book cases from wooden orange boxes. These used to be chopped up for firewood but now Shirley saved them for us. Henry offered to make some new bookshelves in his workshop but these followed much later.

We soon had a small collection of books. Matron was able to help us from outside sources and set aside a small budget for the purchase of some new books. Gradually other patients became interested and Meg arranged a library day each Monday. She was always there to keep an eye on things and the library was kept locked on the other days. Sometimes the books were not returned and it was difficult to trace them but Meg was not unduly concerned. She thought it was better for patients to develop an interest rather than to lay down too many rules and regulations.

"Every book you see here has been somebody's best friend," Meg brushed her hand across the rows of exposed spines. "Between the covers of each of those books lies a boundless universe waiting to be discovered." Some were bound in wine-coloured leather and the gold letters of titles gleamed in the light. I drew near and caressed them with the tips of my fingers.
"I would like to teach you to read", Meg said.

But I knew that learning to read begins very early in life, almost alongside learning to talk. Our house had been devoid of books apart from the little nursery stories which Nana put in our Christmas stockings. I had practically no early education and had always had a yearning to read but I knew that I had left it too late in life. Meg led me to a little stool in the corner. She did what Nana used to do, talked about the pictures and read the words. I didn't know it then, but she had taken me by the hand and given me my first steps in reading. With her background in teaching, she knew that this was where reading began.

"You are sitting there with a look of intense concentration. You know. I think I can make a reader of you, but it's not a case of actual teaching at this stage, just a matter of letting yourself absorb the wonders of the written word and develop an interest in books and learn how to handle and respect a book. You will soon get enjoyment from the written language," she told me.

She began by reading to me and supporting me through the regular sharing of books. It wasn't long before I was ready for the next step. I was particularly keen to learn and began to notice letters and recognise a word or two when we started to read together. It soon meant a means of escape sitting in the little library or in Meg's bedroom.

During this phase I started remembering word patterns and learning about the language of books. This was a very important part for me. "Don't be disheartened," Meg warned me. "It is a very gradual process."

After that each day we would set aside a quiet time with no distractions, ten to fifteen minutes to begin with and then a half hour. She made sure that the sessions were not too long and that I wouldn't get tired or bored, and always made reading an enjoyable experience. She sat patiently with me and never tried to pressurise me if I seemed a bit reluctant. If she thought I was losing interest then she would move on to something else, like a walk out in the fresh air or back to her room for a cup of tea.

The weeks went by quickly and I was already grasping the rudiments of reading. Meg encouraged me to maintain the flow and if I mispronounced a word she did not interrupt immediately, instead allowed me an opportunity for self-correction. She thought it was better to tell me some of the unknown words to maintain the flow rather than insisting on trying to make me build them all up from the sounds of the letters. She was always positive.

Success was the key. Although she was anxious for me to progress she never gave me a book that was too difficult. She knew that this would be counterproductive. "Remember," she said, "Nothing succeeds like success. Read the easy books first."

"Struggling with a book with many unknown words is pointless. You will lose the flow and then you won't understand the text. "Regular practice, that's the secret," she said. "It's like learning to play tennis or any other skill. Little and often is best."

After this, I began to live for my books and my reading had launched me into more carefree conversations with Meg, Shirley, even with Matron and especially with Charles but that was much later.

I worked my way through the children's section and then moved on to the adult shelves. To all outward appearances it was a good time in my life. It was a time of reconstruction of hope, an optimistic and new sort of freedom from fear. My small room became my second library and my books were now my treasures. During the early years after I had learned to read, we spent many evenings debating simple topics. I began to realise that improving my reading could change my life.

Meg tried to sweep me away into the cloudy realms of history and politics but in these fields she soon left me far behind. Then she introduced me to the daily newspaper which lay each morning on Matron's desk in the entrance hall. This helped to update me in current affairs. Through helping me read aloud Meg developed in me a new way of talking more slowly and more distinctly than I had done before with more confidence and more fluency. These were my first steps in picking up reading and the habit stuck with me for the years ahead. I sensed correctly that my world had forever changed. It had been my second retreat after my initial salvation through hard work in the kitchen.

One day we sat in the library and Meg said casually as she stroked a book. "Maybe this is something you will do one day. Put your name on the spine of a book." I just laughed. I didn't think so.

But maybe this is it. I had started writing this story some time after Meg had taught me the rudiments of reading and writing. In fact it was about ten years after we founded out little library and I had read a lot of books and autobiographies by then. I was twenty-six when I first put pen to paper and by then Meg had just celebrated her fiftieth birthday. She sat with me in the evenings and read the first drafts of my story.

I asked her to edit it for me and to make suggestions but she said. "It's your story and you're doing just fine but I do like to read it just to make sure you're not saying anything bad about me, and I don't want any flattery either," she laughed.

I just shook my head and laughed with her. Anything I say about Meg on these pages is not flattery. No words of mine could ever equal her wisdom or do justice to the way she rescued me and brought me out of the depths of despair. Her radiance and her warmth haunted every corner of my life. How I wish she had lived long enough to hold my book in her hands. I could just hear her say, "I told you so." She was one of the very few persons in the world who truly believed in me. I had to admit that becoming an author or anything of that nature was a rather foolish and unrealistic ambition given my background and my limited intelligence.

After that we had discussions about anything and everything. She used to smile, a strange mysterious smile as her thoughts turned in on themselves but I knew what she was thinking. She had taken this young, ignorant girl and begun to fill a space inside her which was begging to be crammed with words and thoughts and ideas and facts and fictions.

As we sat in Meg's bedroom at dusk, the Yorkshire countryside stretched away to the horizon. Soft mist hung in the valleys and the tops of the low hills were gold in the evening sun. I smiled because the whole world was fresh and new and bright. I was raised to a higher level, surrounded by books, making invisible friends in their pages and being plunged into a new world of images and sensations peopled by characters who seemed so real to me.

I realised what I had gained and still remember Meg's words, "We will find contentment if we think more of what life has given us rather than what life has taken away."

Kathy Lavelle

Chapter 11

My former shyness was absorbed into my work. I buried myself in the various activities. "The more physical the better," I thought.

"Hard work," Meg had reminded me "is the best medicine yet devised for all the ills of man or women."

In fact I became less like a patient and more like a member of the permanent staff. They were like my own family and they knew me

I wasn't expecting anything in return, but my hard work in the kitchen had slowly but surely begun to pay off. I had been allocated my small room off the kitchen and crawled at night into my cosy little bed deep in the wall behind the kitchen fire.

I was asked to look out for Angel. In fact, I think just about everybody was looking out for Angel. Gabriel is her real name but she likes to be called Angel ever since she was chosen to be the Angel Gabriel in a Nativity play when she was about five or six years old. She always sat with her hands twisting in her lap, and knees locked tightly together. That was how I saw her in the refectory on that first morning.

I met her one morning walking down the garden path when the snow had turned to slush underfoot and a keen wind blew through the trees. She seemed quite oblivious of the weather conditions and she never dressed warmly. Angel had shoulder-length, straw-coloured hair and timid green eyes which appeared permanently startled. Her thin wrists and forearm were prominently veined.

And the first time I saw her in the snow, I opened my eyes wide with panic thinking she was an apparition. Her pale face was standing out against the dark and when she moved towards me her face was shining white against the sun. The fragile skin of her bony limbs glowed against the brown of the faces of others. Her hair was like silk tumbling in beautiful waves over her shoulders and glistening in the early morning light.

"Have you ever seen a child who looks so angelic?" Shirley used to ask.

She had a girlish lightness, a delicate, little creature, swaying and willowy, light and graceful of movement. It never seemed to me that she walked, just glided along.

One day in the kitchen when we hadn't been talking about anything in particular, Shirley was looking through her menus and I was dusting the shelves.

"Angel murdered her pimp," Shirley said all of a sudden. "She had been working as a prostitute for a number of months at the time of his death. Apparently her pimp had been her lover but he used to beat her up and then bring her gifts to humour her. He had been violent towards her and they frequently argued, the disputes mainly over money, but in the end his violence cost him his life. She could take no more of the beatings and apparently had stabbed him with a kitchen knife. The following morning she claimed to have found his body. Her lawyer got her off on the grounds of self-defence and diminished responsibility."

"Shh! Kathy doesn't want to hear this, we have heard that story so many times," Meg whispered.

"Don't let it bother you dear. She is quite harmless," Shirley said. "The only damage she is doing is to herself. Because she thinks she is an angel, she has the impression she should be slim and graceful. She suffers from an eating disorder."

Angel looked about fourteen years old, but her mind was outside time. It seemed as though early dementia had set in. She didn't go out a lot, didn't talk much, and didn't think much as far as I could tell. She stayed lost somewhere in the middle of her own world. I often wondered if it was worth envying her for that kind of peace. She had a permanent smile on her face but sometimes her smile faded into a look of intense sadness.

I sat with Meg until quite late one evening and she told me many stories about Angel and how hard everyone had worked on trying to get her to eat. She was harmless and the doctors felt she could be reunited with her family but she had to stay on for treatment.

I told Meg about my own fears and struggles.

"We must keep striving within ourselves and out of all this horror something good will come.
You're doing a great job. In fact you are stronger than you think," Meg said. "Be strong. Tough times never last but tough people do."

Meg had been my strength and Shirley a fountain of knowledge, not just on the history of mental institutions but world history and current affairs.   One morning when Shirley was washing the vegetables, she told me about the   bizarre and savage practices of mad-doctors. That's what she called psychiatrists. She described how in the olden days they treated those afflicted with manias ranging from huge doses of opium, blood-letting and cold-water immersion to beatings and confinements in cages. She said, "The care of the mentally sick was riddled with sadism and embezzlement and if that wasn't dehumanising enough, jeering, sightseers were permitted entry into the asylums for a fee."

"It's not Angel you have to worry about," Shirley said one morning when we were sitting having our cup of tea.

"One patient they need to worry about is Nick. He is a violent criminal who had been sent to Broadmoor high-security psychiatric hospital but after only three years he had been transferred to this place, claiming he was cured. I can never understand why. More than once, security staff have come upon scenes of violence."

He had a villainous cut-throat face. It was probably the scar that made him look that way, it started by the corner of his mouth and ran along the bottom of his left cheek almost to his neck. His black, uncombed hair stood out on end in all directions.

"He is a selfish and ruthless man and a domestic tyrant," Shirley said. "He endured cruelty from his father and is now casting his own frightening shadow over the earth."

Shirley seemed to know the background to every patient and promised to tell me more about Nick later.

"People have tried to warn those in authority but they won't listen. Mark my words, they will have blood on their hands if they don't have him transferred back to a secure institution."

They said he had been cured and could survive in this asylum with the right medication and constant supervision. He was considered to be a reformed character but Shirley had other ideas. We saw for ourselves, through the kitchen window, that everyone's nerves were on edge in the men's exercise yard when he was around and arguments would break out over the slightest thing. He had no sympathy for anyone, not even cripples or old people.

"Once he had twenty electric shock treatments," Shirley told us. "But he just walked around talking and talking, raving, and breaking things, furniture, pictures off the wall, dishes everything.   Two wardens had hold of him, one on each arm."

One afternoon, during the exercise period, I saw him, from the window, whirling about in circles and shouting in a frantic way before the eyes of the horrified crowds who just stood there with faces frozen with horror. He walked up to one of the new male patients, grabbed him by the shirt collar, lifted him up off his feet and began banging his head on the wall. The poor man's head was battered, bloodied and bruised, with bright red blood spurting from his nose and mouth, one eye was swollen shut, and later after an X-ray, they discovered he had three broken ribs.

 "You are in serious trouble, now just keep calm," one of the wardens said.   They were already dragging Nick towards the building but he sat down on the ground and started sobbing uncontrollably, shouting, sobbing like a baby, while some of the patients laughed and made fun of him. As they tried to dose him up on tranquilisers, he lost his temper and managed to push one of the wardens away while the other inmates continued to shout and kick up terrifying hysterical outbursts.

"You've had it. It's back to the lockup for you."

Chapter 12

Meg was twenty-four years older than I was but sometimes she looked a lot younger. At night-time, she let her hair down and it streamed over her shoulders.

She had told me about herself, about her own work as a schoolteacher; about her early marriage, her lovely little Anna and I began to have sympathy for her. I was not the only one with problems. When I ended up telling her my story, she had listened and she was not shocked, nor even scared of the burden this might put on our friendship.

I told her about my recurring dreams and when I had finished I was shaking. "The horror is still with me," I said, "and it will never go away."

"In my nightmares," I told her, "my memory constantly takes me back along the muddy paths between the brambles and heather."

"Last night I could see Johnny from the path but I was far away from him, my heart beating wildly. Almost falling for lack of balance. I was worried about my legs. I couldn't seem to control them. Dusk had fallen, with strange streaks of light across the sky where the sun had gone down behind the black clouds. I followed on quickly down to the bottom field and straight over the stone wall tumbling a couple of times and heaving myself up. I could see him through a crack in the wall."

"I lay still and took shallow breaths. Every inch of my skin pricked and burned. I started back to the farm. I knew the puppies would need a feed. I was shivering uncontrollably. It was cold, a bitter cold combined with fear and exhaustion, which made me shake from head to toe. But there he was right in front of me. He pulled me forward by my skirt until my body was up against his. He drew my head back and looked at me. I began to cry, "Please don't," I pleaded but I was crushed into the ground. The rough heather cut me on my back and tears came out of the corners of my eyes and rolled down either cheek.

"I'll kill you if you scream." His voice was manic, unrecognisable. I remained motionless.
"Do you understand? If you scream you're dead." I nodded my head. I was suddenly frantic. I was trapped like a frightened

animal. His smell was nauseating and clung to my skin long afterwards. And then I woke up."

I broke down in sobs.

"Shh. Take it easy. Next time you have a nightmare, just come to me or knock on the wall and I will come into your room. But remember, he can't hurt you anymore."

Chapter 13

I lay on my little bed in the dimming light but there were too many memories crowding in on me. I wanted to push out the bad ones and concentrate on the better times.

My story began in happier days, in a springtime long ago in a world of birdsong and bleating lambs. My mind flashed back more than a decade when I was fifteen and I roamed the hillside with Michael. We did everything together. It is curious to me how I remember so completely the feel of the wind in my hair. Recently Michael began to loom largely in my dreams. Some of the old nightmares were beginning to fade. I see Michael standing there by the river, holding my hand as I crossed gingerly to the other side across the little slatted bridge.

I wanted to forget the gruesome things, madness and mad doctors. The green hills were in my mind with Michael lifting the new-born lambs and sometimes letting me hold one. There is something special in the air, some new optimism with the new life of spring. Maybe it is to do with the sun too, back again after weeks of cloudy skies or maybe things I remember about Michael, rock solid, caring, predictable and always in control, always knowing what to do. I knew he loved me and dreamed that one day he would marry me and would stay true and we would have children of our own. We walked through a carpet of dazzling blue in the mottled sunlight of the woods.

The bluebells flourished at that time of year, my favourite wildflowers with their delicate aroma. I would pick a bunch to bring back to Nana who always placed them in a jam jar on the kitchen window. My dreams carried me back to these treasured times of my life, such times are burned clearly and sharply on my mind.

On the farm everything was done according to plan. There are rules for everything and schedules to be met, guidelines to be followed in the grand cycle of events. The evening sky was beginning to lighten bringing those positive sensations. The sparkling water reflected the setting sun, the long stalks of iris plants were coming along the river banks and I was reliving so many happy memories. I pictured myself walking through the narrow paths as the shadows stretched out in the dying light.

Michael was a couple of months older than I was but much wiser. There was only a steep valley dividing his farm from ours. The ground was soft and wet, the trees intertwined their branches overhead as I took off my shoes, and stepped into the water   I can see the water rushing between large rocks but Michael, with his youthful energy, is holding my hand and again we are back at the other side. He led me across the blue bridge and down towards the cascading waters of the weir. He would be big now, tall with muscles, much more a man than a boy of sixteen. There would never be anyone else like him in my life. That's what I thought in those days.

He had promised to marry me when he was older. "Won't people think we are such a fine pair, so well-suited? I'll have my own farm one day and make real money, enough to build a house for us and help my mother and father too," he used to say with such confidence.   Bluebells still remind me of him and I think it's funny how their delicate perfume can do that, taking me straight back to that carefree place, reminding me of so much happiness.

At that time I had the same dreams of Michael over and over,   his arms around me and his body so familiar to me as if all this time I had kept some living copy of it in my mind.

Chapter 14

It was one of the most exciting days of our lives and a major landmark when television sets were installed in the asylum, not just one, but a large TV set in each of the two main common rooms and two smaller sets, one in Matron's quarters and one for the kitchen staff located in Shirley's sitting room. The arrival of the TV made a radical change to our daily routines both for patients and staff. Meal times were made to coincide with favourite programmes and often menus had to be adjusted to create space for the kitchen staff in the evenings. Shirley turned over the new page of the calendar on the kitchen notice board. Everyone knew it was the big day. Crowds clustered around the television screens which were located in the common rooms. Now everyone was staring at the flickering grey of the screen when the first programme came on.

Matron's idea was that, "It can't do any harm and will keep the patients quiet for a few hours especially in the winter evenings."

But it didn't always work out that way. Sometimes arguments broke out about the characters on the screen or about people talking during a broadcast. It was funny but when a fight broke out on the screen, certain patients in particular became violent. It seemed to be a springboard for their aggression. Then they would all be sent back to their rooms and the sets switched off. The fighting sometimes carried on in the exercise yards or on the corridors and often wardens had to be called in and the main offenders frogmarched off to cells or given a warning.

Everyone was immediately drawn to the programmes and sat huddled together. You could hear a pin drop and anyone who broke the silence was removed immediately. The wardens were as keen as we were and sat along the sides of the room keeping an eye on any offenders. We sat there in silence watching, absorbing every word.

The popularity of the TV never diminished. There was still a rush for the chairs in front of the television sets after supper. They watched the highlights of their favourite programmes that everyone looked forward to and talked about throughout the day. People were so engrossed that sometimes they forgot to go to the toilets which were situated at the end of the long corridor. There was one night I particularly remembered when in the middle of an enthralling story, Daphne, a very old woman, was found sitting in a pool of her own urine. There were noisy protests and she let out a loud groan when the nurse hoisted her into a contraption that would wheel her to the bathroom.

But the attraction wasn't just the films. I began to learn more about life in the county. I watched farming programmes and the daily news. Life outside was changing drastically. I soon learned that it was a very different situation for women in those changing days, things improving all the time. Women seemed to be given a greater voice and were becoming recognised for their contribution to industry and to politics. And even inside there were changes, well for me anyway. My concern had been to help find some niche where I could be happy or at least content and I think I had found it. I had never asked much of life and I had now begun to write my story of survival. I was happy then but I never thought I would see the outside world again. The television brought the outside world into our narrow existence and I was content in my own way. I felt we were living with people on the other side of the globe.

Shirley praised me at the end of every session in the kitchen and I knew the complements were sincere. But I was surrounded by a variety of people less fortunate than I was, some very strange and contrary, often brutally treated or denied privileges. Their rooms were lofty, scantily furnished with unreliable heating at that time. It was always a long winter and even at the end of March it had still been bitterly cold. The faces of most of the inmates, were pale, their eyes dull, resigned, weighed down with a certain sadness and worry. But I had my cosy little room, an escape into books and into a world of my own.

Chapter 15

One evening around this time, Shirley sent me down to the shoemaker's with a large bag of boots and shoes. I wandered towards the workshop at the back of the building and came upon old Gerry the shoemaker, or cobbler as he was called in those days. This is where our shoes were sent for repairs.

This brought me back to the days when, as a young girl, I was sent to the village to have our shoes repaired and was amazed by the array of shoes in Mark Smith's little word room. There were plain black, sturdy, lace up shoes with leather uppers and leather soles. Our shoes were always leather in those days and as far as I remember synthetic shoes had not yet appeared on the market, at least not in my village. I clearly remember the times they were taken to the cobbler. That was an adventure in itself. Mark's room was a blend of the most unusual smells, the new leather, the oil from the black, greasy sewing machine and smells of glue mingling with that of the waxed hemp.

His tiny workshop had rows of shelves containing shoes in all shapes and sizes, ranging from the tiny baby's shoe resting on the smallest last to men's brogues battered and scuffed from farm or factory, to ladies pointed toes, elegant once but now gnarled and misshapen by bunions and twisted toes. Even then style came before comfort. When we entered Mark's little work room, the bench was crowded with a clutter of small hammers and large rounded hammers, lasts in various sizes, lengths of waxed hemp, half-moon knives and sole knives, tacks and pincers, curved awls and straight awls.

Lengths of waxed hemp hung from the wall on long nails. Shaping irons sat on the fire and remnants of leather littered the floor but the greatest attraction was the pot-bellied stove in the corner. It was always red hot like smelted iron. Nana loved to sit near the stove and listen to Mark, bent over his bench in his old felt hat, telling joke after joke as he whittled away at the leather and hammered neat rows of rivets around the sole of the shoe. We often had to wait until the repairs were carried out as we didn't have another pair. He placed the shoes on the last, which sat upside down on the lasting jack, and nailed the thick leather sole in place. The nails were clinched inside with the metal cobbler's foot. Then he sat on his high bench with the shoe placed between his knees, whittling the edges of the leather, before polishing and waxing the uppers. The new soles and heels were in place and the uppers shone like they were brand new as he proudly presented them to us.

But there were no fancy shoes in the asylum. They were all made from sturdy, black leather and repaired over and over again. It was a different way of life and my mind transported me back to the hillside, the wild goats and the wind-tossed rooks. It was the place I had once called home and suddenly it was all there before my eyes. I thought then that I could never return.

I knew that on the day I was snatched away from it and through all the years I had tried to put it from my mind and mostly I had succeeded until something as simple as a cobbler's workshop had brought it all back to me.

Gerry took the bag of shoes from me. "You look good today. What's a pretty girl like you doing in a place like this?" I smiled and felt just a little uncomfortable. "I'll be back when they are ready," I said and made my way towards the door but Gerry was there before me. The door was closed and just then he grabbed me and pressed me up against the wall with all the weight of his body pressing against me. I panicked. My whole nightmare had returned.

Just then I heard a voice. "Are you in there Kathy?" It was Shirley come to the rescue.

Gerry sprang towards the door and opened it. "She's just coming. I'll get these done as soon as I can Shirley."

Shirley could see my body was trembling and took me back up to the kitchen.

"He's had a pass at you. Hasn't he? I shouldn't have sent you down there. I'm so sorry love. In his younger days, he was quite a womaniser but Matron knew I could handle him."

Shirley reached for the kettle and said, "And you know something, he is not one of us. He is a paid member of staff. It would be impossible to get one of the inmates with skills like that and anyway a cobbler's workshop is full of lethal instruments. They couldn't take the risk. But Gerry has behaved himself for the past twenty years. Whatever has come over him?"

I knew then of his reputation but it was never spoken of again.

Chapter 16

One night I awoke with a start and it took me a while to work out where I was. In the blackness I could hear the sound of the wind playing havoc with the barbed wire on the high walls. Around me the house slept, the old pipes moaned and the floorboards creaked. I listened. I couldn't move. The wind was whipping up and the farm gate was rocking on its posts. I had dreamt that dream again and it was still with me when I woke. The mournful hollow sound of an owl hooted and I felt suddenly lonely and scared. There was a sharp cry from one of the locked cells above and a muttering in the corridor. An anguished cry sounded from somewhere outside and I sat up trembling in the dim light. The noise of the water down at the wharf, crashed against the pillars. Then in the storm I saw a figure. I screamed out to whoever it was, screamed and screamed. Johnny was watching me in the rain. When I ate my meals, or drank or lay down to sleep he was there in front of me. I peered anxiously, listening carefully for a laugh or cough to help me regain my composure.

But all I saw was a mighty thickness of heather and bracken and jutting rocks where I stumbled in the dark, tripping over a stub of tree trunk jutting out of the ground, stumbling forward all over the path until I righted myself. Then I tripped on a coil of rusted wire which mangled and tore my dress with a great gaping hole down one side. The rain lashed across in front of me. The storm had closed about me again.

Then I remembered that once when I was very small on a winter's day, Uncle Johnny had carried me home from the fair inside his jacket buttoned up so close that I felt warm and secure and safe from all harm. It was about ten years later when I ran from him panting, scratched by brambles, my feet catching every root, every rough stone on the path, every tangled branch until I reached the gate at the bottom wall where I stopped and stumbled forwards to where the river widened and bubbled over the rocks. I stood up and waded across safely to the other side, out of his reach. It was always Johnny who dominated my nightmares, and I see my face and body become swollen and bruised when he leapt on me like a wild animal.

Later, Nana helped me undress and got me some dry clothes and a high-necked jumper to hide the scratches on my neck. But she was too terrified to speak out. She had been threatened so many time of being sent to the workhouse. She got me a basin of hot water and I carefully washed my face and lips, my arms and thighs, and every part of my body taking care not to miss a single inch going over it several times with soap and water. Only Nana knew how scared I was and consoled me in my solitude. To me she was a guardian angel. I would give anything to have her now, just to console me and tell me that things will be all right in the end.

Afterwards I was suddenly lost for words, withdrawn into myself, my innocence gone. On Sunday morning the terror of it all roared in my ears. Then the silence came and followed me into the cold echoing church back in my village. Kneeling down in the bright beams of sunshine from the stain-glass windows, I wanted to hold my arms outstretched towards the beam of light. I remember it all so clearly, but why did I feel so dirty and ashamed? I closed my eyes and I wanted to scream but I was in the house of God.

Nana sat beside me. "Are you all right?" she whispered. She looked at me and I felt a great sadness because there was such emptiness in her eyes. She was carrying the burden of my pain. It had always been our delight to go to the service on the feast of the Annunciation, but this year was very different. I remember the scene so well, the small church filled with candles on the side altar, the light of the candles illuminating Fr Lynch's face as he stood in the pulpit all smiles and gushing with piety, the essence of goodness. I shivered at the memory. This was before I knew what he really was. I gazed all around, into the line faces, to the mosaics on the floor and the walls of the church, into the voice of Father Lynch. The choir began to sing some forgotten hymn. What would I give to be back in that church, but back before those fateful days? I wanted to put everything back the way it was before it was broken.

After the Sunday service Johnny bought me sweets and a doll in the village store, like I was a child. I was fifteen now and because of him, I had lost my innocence but he gave me presents for my silence. At other times he would make lewd comments about my body whenever we were alone. Mother never noticed how much I avoided him and put my distant moods down to puberty. I was still convinced she wouldn't believe the truth. But it continued to haunt me. The moment it was dark I became bitterly cold but the peat fire warmed our little house. In the midst of the howling storm I found a comforting place in Nana's room and went to sleep with my little sister Rosie curled in my arms.

When Dad heard about my pregnancy, his anger boiled over. He slapped me across the face and thumped me into the bedroom. "Wait till I get my hands on that Michael Wilson," he said. "If he ever darkens this place again, he's dead."

I wanted to scream out, "It wasn't Michael. It was your beloved brother Johnny." In those days the very fact of illegitimacy deprived me of an identity. The thought haunted me. If I should have a child what would the outcome be? What I didn't know then was that I would be mysteriously removed from my home through the conniving of my Dad and Father Lynch and Johnny. On one occasion Dad came into my bedroom and hit me all over with his belt, then turned around and slammed the door furiously behind him. The thought came crashing through me that it would be better not to be born at all than to be born to such a father. I had seen my mother falling to the ground from the blows of his monstrous hand. He was a drunk and a bully but poor Nana knew to avoid his anger. He had threatened so often that he would get rid of her, but these were idle threats. She was a useful member of the household.

I distinctly remember one particular day my Dad pushed me off the chair.
"Get up you lazy, good-for-nothing wench and give Johnny the seat and put the kettle on."

Johnny looked at me with a smirk and casually walked over and took my seat. Dad's anger was always stirring deep inside him like a volcano spewing hatred and anger everywhere he went and his presence loomed up like a ghostly tyrant revelling in his tyrannical power over us.

I woke myself crying out, "Meg, Meg." A tentative knock sounded on the door, and Meg appeared. She crept into the small bed beside me and held me tightly in her arms.

"Shh, Shh, it's only a bad dream." We both went back to sleep in each other arms until the first rays of light cast shadows over the wall.

Kathy Lavelle

Chapter 17

It was a good day. I carried Nana's photo with me in my apron pocket. Her spirit was always with me. She entered my head and filled my thoughts and spun around me and danced through me until it felt like we were together again never to be parted. She restored my courage and I felt like a fighter again. I was now more like a member of the permanent staff than a patient, dashing around in the kitchen, knowing all the doctors, nurses and orderlies as if they were my own family and they all treated me with respect. I began to think if I had to stay here all my life, I could tolerate it. I could even enjoy it. "I have had a lot of luck," I told myself, "to have had such a good life here. Now at last I am no longer angry."

I sat in Meg's little room and she was speaking calmly. "You could certainly write a book when you get through with all this. Now is a good time to continue telling your story."

"Yes I will think about it," I knew it would please Meg if I made the effort especially after all she had done for me. At least I would go through the motions. But from what I had written so far, I wasn't sure I had the vocabulary to articulate my story but Meg had played a valuable part in my survival and I owed it to her to give it another try. At long last I could make an effort to put my education to some use. Meg had taught me well and I had read a lot of the books in our new library, but as soon as I had finished them, more and more books came pouring in, gifts from places like Church bazaars and school garden fetes.

I know that the retelling of history can never be perfect especially when the piecing together of the story has been done by a person with as modest an intellect as myself. Much of my life before this point in time is hazy and therefore may appear to be of little interest to anyone.

"Mine is a sad and secret story." I told Meg.

"Yes but it would be therapeutic. Isn't that a good enough reason to think seriously about continuing to write it."

"Okay, I will go back to the beginning and write as quickly as I can."

"That's the spirit."

Meg told me that "All writing is capturing sights and thoughts on paper. It will help you shake off the grey skies. We need to search backwards from the vantage point of the present to appraise things in the past and attribute meaning to them. A good story has a beginning, a middle and an end. A good page-turner and it's over. That's all there is to it!"

"Well, it isn't as easy as that. For one thing there isn't an end in sight." I knew what she meant, to get to the point and write the most important things. But I knew there was a certain way of telling and it would take time to tell. After all it had taken me ten years to begin so I had to do it in my own way.

"It's not as easy as you think," I told myself " and I still don't know why I have agreed to write it."

The days passed peacefully. Meg and I went to the evening service in the chapel. The service had already started but my mind was whirling around thinking of my story, what I would put in and more importantly what I would leave out. Meg nudged me and I suddenly sat up and started paying attention. The vicar was climbing the steps into the pulpit. He was preaching a sermon about the gift of hope and about giving your pain to God. We came away spiritually refreshed and wandered into Shirley's kitchen. No matter what time it was, day or night, she was always there doing something.

We sat around the table for hot drinks and a light supper. The radio was on and we let Elvis and Chuck Berry and Buddy Holly fill the air.

"Life isn't too bad," Shirley said as she passed the cakes around.

Chapter 18

I had heard so much about Charles, the new psychiatrist and was smiling in sheer anticipation of meeting him for the first time. From the kitchen I could see his car arriving. On this particular morning, a storm was moving in. Each time the lightning flashed, it illuminated the interior of the kitchen with an oddly harsh light throwing Shirley's face into sharp relief. "Glory be to god," she said making a cross over her forehead. "It's the only thing I am scared of."

Another blaze of lightening flashed across the sky, then another and another in quick succession. There was screaming down the corridor. Shirley had disappeared into the darkness of her small office. There was no window and she considered it a safe haven in the storm. Lightning flashed again. The thunder came more quickly this time. The storm was getting closer. I wasn't scared of the storm but was afraid of the emotion inside me, confusion, elation, fear and anticipation. I hoped it wasn't showing on my face.

I knocked, was invited in. "Nice to see you Kathy," Charles said softly as he took my hand. He was sitting in his shirt sleeves, a very handsome young man, but he wasn't reading all that medical jargon like Dr. Mac. He started by making general easy chitchat, asking me about this and that to put me at my ease.

Charles was looking into my eyes calmly. It was as though he knew my needs and understood my background and wanted to help me. He looked through my notes but every few moments he glanced up at me, away from the files and smiled reassuringly. Slowly I relaxed and began to be at ease with myself.

My nerves melted away leaving me calm and totally relaxed. He made it so easy to speak. I let it all spill out. I wanted him to take me in his arms and say, "It's ok. It's all over now. I will take care of you." But we were as different as night and day when it came to independence and self-confidence. A short silence followed and then more gentle questions. Charles gave me hope for a heart-stopping instant.

Chapter 19

I knew in my heart that everything was beautiful again as they handed me my baby. I heard him so clearly, a little muffled sound.

"What is his name?" Nana was standing smiling beside me.

"I'm calling him Tommy," I said.

But in the small hours of the night I awoke to the sound of a little banging somewhere, probably a sound I had heard a million times before, a door in the house that knocks against its frame in the draught.

The gloom gradually brightened or my eyes adjusted to it. I got dressed and I was a little warmer now even though it was the coldest day of the year so far. Shirley had given me extra blankets. I was still caught in a dream and just for a moment thought I saw a little figure standing by my bed. Nana! I'm sure it was. She had come to tell me that things were all right now. After a while I went back to sleep until the clock struck six. The dream had kept something alive in me, the flowing of the shining silver river through the granite hills, winding its way to the open sea. I would lie on my bed and listen to a delivery van coming up the drive, listen to the clock tick in that absolute stillness, and eventually gave way to easy slumber and happier dreams.

Shirley was always in the warm kitchen waiting for us. She was busy with early-morning preparations and singing along with the latest hit on the radio. She looked up from her work and when she saw me she came and held my hand.

"My goodness, you are freezing. Come and have a hot drink."

When we both got into the swing of the morning routine, we started talking in low tones as we always did. Now and again Shirley's eyes lighted with a glint of amusement over something I had said or something she had heard on the radio. Today she talked about the Asylum.

"I still don't know why people like you and me had been incarcerated here for our whole lives without any just cause," Shirley said. "The doctors said I was here for my own protection but I'm not so sure. I know we have settled here but I sometimes wonder what it would be like on the other side."

"I was also told by a doctor, no, by Father Lynch that it was for my own protection. He said that people like me were not good at reading the intentions of others, and could therefore be victimised,"

"Umm! These people are gods onto themselves," she said. "But some of them are having it coming to them."

I had recognised an inner loneliness in her that matched my own. She always said, "Some things are just too difficult to talk about."

But then she started to open up a little. She trembled and then her trembling changed into low timid suppressed sobs. She knelt down and laid her head on a seat and cried and cried. We just sat there, one crying the other consoling.
"I had a son. He would be your age now if he had lived. His name was Jack. The doctor said, "If he lives, he will be brain damaged." Then they stuck a needle in him. And that was that. I went mad when they lowered his little white coffin into an enormous grave. It was raining and two men had to hold me back. They thought I was going to jump into the grave after Jack. I blamed the doctor and arguments went on for a long time. Then they locked me up for the rest of my life. My husband was already having an affair with another woman, one of my best friends, so he wasn't much support!"

I just sat there with my arm around her shoulders.

But Shirley was soon back in her happy mood, playing live music on her transistor radio and listening to her daily episode of the Archers. One morning she announced, "It is 1963, the space age they're calling it. A man has circled the earth in a rocket. And do you know, they've invented a pill so married women don't have to get pregnant? And the TV is telling us about soldiers getting killed in Vietnam. What is the world coming to?"

Later, Shirley got back onto the subject of injustices in mental institutions. "Charles hears it every day. And he is not turning a blind eye to it. Things are going to change around here. Injustices have been done to too many for too long."

"But then of course there are the real madmen, people like Nick. He should be locked up in a more secure unit. He's not getting the help he needs and he's a danger to everyone here. People keep telling Matron that he needs help, counselling and anger management and maybe a special psychiatrist who deals with people like him. They treat us as though we have all got the same problems. He definitely needs specialist help which he is not getting and I worry about what is going to happen one of these days."

"But on the other side of the coin there's Angel, poor little dear. She has been offered all the help she needs but she wants nothing to do with the other patients or the doctors. She has such limited contact with people, just at meals really and eats nothing, or occasionally in the library but reads nothing. I can't see why she wants to go there. They have done numerous psychological tests, and they have boxes of notes on her case but they are not giving her any practical help. Presumably they are not fully aware of her background and the danger she is to herself. At first, because of the nature of her case and the publicity around it they kept her apart from other patients but now they don't think she is a threat to anyone. She runs around like a child instead of staying in control of her situation. You have seen her leaving her food untouched, and she remains wide awake the whole night through. Sometimes the warden observers her as she sits staring vacantly into space for hours. She exercises alone and doesn't join in group activities of any sort."

I agreed with Shirley. "She needs more help with her anorexia and it is impossible to get close to her but what can we do? She's friendly with everyone and yet she has no friends, I have tried to help her but she just runs off laughing like a child."

"We have just got to keep working on it as best we can but it is impossible to help some people."

"All the same we have come a long way in the treatment of mental illnesses," Shirley went on. Sometimes when she got on her soap box, you had no idea where it would lead. "Take this building. We have got a park and gardens, and lavish, well kept grounds. These are intended to be therapeutic and to help cure the patients, to give some element of freedom. Treatment is now based on kindness and keeping us occupied or is supposed to be. We have the new central administration block containing the Medical Superintendent's residence with doctors on call day and night."

"And another thing! Did you know that we are offered compensation with an annual pension? This is put away earning interest so that when we are released we have some money to start a new life. That is some joke."

"I have been reading an article by Professor Hoffman," she said. "He wants to write a comparative study about the old and the new asylums. I'm quite interested in that. In the old Victorian Asylums people were needlessly locked up and badly treated. They were also effective at restricting visitors but nonetheless they were considered to have benevolent and compassionate facilities for vulnerable people. There were similarities between the place for the mad and a place for the aristocrat, elevated and elegant mansions surrounded by extensive grounds and gardens but inside the asylum the rooms were cold and gloomy, often very basic food in the larders and no proper heating. After a century or more of service nearly all Victorian asylums have now closed and their sites and buildings have been sold for property development."

Chapter 20

The advantages at that time were that that we could meet and communicate with the other workers, the gardener, farmers, carpenters, sports leaders and a range of others who all seemed to enjoy their work and often went around whistling or telling jokes. I learned a lot from these people.

One cold winter evening when storm clouds darkened the sky, I walked towards the vegetable plots, and through the high gate. I stood there in front of the blacksmith's forge. Another vision from my childhood flashed through my mind. I remembered the first time my mother took me to the old forge in the centre of our village. She needed some sort of a door hinge fixed.

This forge here was similar but on a much bigger scale. It catered for the large number of farm horses and I tentatively looked in the door. Mark beckoned for me to come further inside. I gazed in awe around the darkened forge with its enormous fireplace and the tools scattered in the corner. It seemed the perfect escape from the cold and rain and I now took a nostalgic look at the irons, pokers, tongs and anvil. Mark lifted the red hot horseshoe out of the fire and moulded it into shape on the large anvil which was his workbench. He punched the holes in the red hot horseshoe for the nails, all the time holding it on his tongs. Then it bubbled and sizzled as he held it into the slack tub to cool. But my favourite bit was when the farmer brought in the horse and Mark held the horse's foot between his legs and started to pare the hoof. He could see that my fascination was growing. "Although we use a lot of tractors nowadays, we still have quite a few horses to pull hay floats and carts carrying goods from one place to another," Mark told me.

I stood there in the darkened forge with tears in my eyes. They had been such happy days, running around the village, such freedom! In and out of the blacksmith's forge, skipping ropes and swings on the green! All day out in the fresh air and into the warmth of the forge in the cool of the evening.

When I went back into the kitchen, Shirley returned to her favourite topic, comparing the old Victorian Asylums to a new changed way of life. Sometimes I thought she read too much or listened to too many history programmes on the wireless.

She was off again. "It's clear that sophisticated diagnoses, better medication and other treatments bring relief to some patients." But my own experiences had not been so positive. I thought back to my first visit to Dr. Mac's surgery.

"A new kind of mind doctor has come into being, maybe because of Freud," Shirley said as she looked towards me. "Don't' you still have your hopes and dreams and the idea of waking up one morning to be told you are free to leave. I'll let you in on a secret. Tomorrow Charles is coming again. Yesterday Matron brought him in here for a cuppa and he was quite at home at my kitchen table. No airs and graces. Just sat there where you're sitting at the kitchen table,"

I had no idea of the profound change Charles would have on my life. I went into his office with the same feelings as on the previous occasion. He was quiet and a good listener, scrolling up and down his notes. The old doctors did all the talking. I still felt the same about Charles but I regained enough composure to answer his questions. He nodded his head to show that he didn't want to press me or hear anything that I wasn't ready to tell him of my own accord. I began to explain the sequence of events that had led to my incarceration. It was such a relief to get it out, like a cleansing of my soul although Meg had kept reminding me I had done nothing wrong. There was patience in his eyes that replaced my own panic and confusion about my feelings for him.

He looked at his notes again. "I am doing my best to find out more about the person who has put you here. I can see nothing to justify it now."

I sat there thinking of my writing. My story is not linear. My mind flashes back and forth in time. It looks like Charles is about to add another chapter to my book. Everything I have written so far is strange because I feel like a visitor from another planet.

Charles was still speaking, "You are not insane. The mad people, the evil people are those out there, the evil ones who testified against you, who took away your freedom. They are the evil ones but I promise you that justice will be done."

I thanked him and wanted to linger as he held my hand. He had brought a new dignity into the place and now he was giving me renewed hope.

Meg put a protective hand on the small of my back as her steered me through the corridor after my appointment. I walked through the door into a different world from the one I had seen yesterday. I could hear a bird singing in the twilight. We walked down the garden path and sat beneath the green arch of trees. Darkness began to creep around us and with it the chill of the winter evening. I had started to burn off some of the negative energy and it felt good sitting there bathed in the evening light.

The next few days passed in a strange kind of calm. I had been carrying the heavy burden of horror and despair, but now the much lighter feeling of hope.

Kathy Lavelle

Chapter 21

Meg's hands were now wrung with arthritis and her thin face was pale and slightly drawn. We wandered out into the spring sunshine and she took hold of my hand and led me to a bench in the shade of the old chestnut tree. She commented on how the gardens were bright with spring blossoms and splattered with daffodils and crocuses. We had found refuge in the foliage which surrounded the bench where we sat in our little sanctuary. The orchards were bright with apple blossoms and almond and cherry blossoms surrounded by vivid fuchsia hedges

Meg asked me how I felt. "Last night I lay on my stomach burying my face into my pillow, waiting for the tears to start but they didn't. This was one of my better nights for a long time," I told her.

"Good girl," she said. "Whatever life throws at you, be strong. I can see you are getting there."

"You must never undervalue yourself. I think you're the kind of person who can excel at anything when you want to or when you have to," she said.

Her face was aglow with light. I held her arm for a moment. It was thin under the white linen of her blouse. I knew then that Meg wasn't well and was steadily losing weight. She hadn't complained but I knew by the things she said that she wasn't her old self. The light was casting a white halo around her entire body. She smiled and the glow around her was like one of those pictures of saints in the church. As she coughed her thin body arched over. I gave her a tissue and she frowned and dabbed at her mouth.

Meg didn't often talk about her own story but today she was remembering how she had been cast out from the world, betrayed by her brother-in-law.

"But I can't say he looked like a villain. He had a calm nature but in those days people were scared of what the neighbours thought. My brother-in-law was a director of a large company and didn't want his reputation put into jeopardy. It was all because of his own good name that he conspired against me. He took it upon himself to question my sanity. That is why I have been here until this day. Never a word from him or anyone else in his family! I would never want to go back. But the irony is that people are getting away with murder nowadays with a much shorter sentence. I read in the paper about a man who punched another man to death and got ten years, maybe even less for good behavior and here we are innocent victims paying a lifetime for someone else's crime. There are secret crimes that go unpunished, crimes that no one has ever recorded or remembered. But I will leave them all to God. I have made a new life for myself here. And believe me I have more friends here than I could ever have outside. No, this is where I will stay until my dying day." There was a wistful look in her eyes.

"That won't be for a long time," I assured her and wished I could have thought of something to cheer her up, the way she had done for me so many times before. It is curious to me how I remember the feel of that evening. I wasn't exactly a girl but I wasn't old either. I had begun to smile again, to eat the meals they gave me. Meg had told me to stay cheerful and to keep up my strength. She had been sent into this world to rescue me.

Her long hair streaked with gray was now tangled and matted, not like it used to be and her eyes had sunken deep into their sockets. I knew she wasn't the person she had been.

We talked about roots. "We have planted new roots here. Yes think about it. For me it's as good an alternative as anything and I'm serving people with real needs. I lost everything," she hesitated, "my husband and baby," her eyes clouded over, "and I would never have started a new life outside. But for you it's different. You are still young. You will be released one day and go on with your life." I knew Meg was talking as though she knew her life was nearing its end.

Suddenly we both noticed there was a little crouched figure there in the corner. It was Angel. She looked more fragile and emaciated than ever, still wearing her dress made of fine silk and chiffon. She was watching us as though she wanted to come over and join us, her dress spread around her, reaching down to the ground. We had all tried so hard but she had become completely withdrawn. She was like a girl from a fairy tale, beautiful with long blonde hair. Meg got up quietly and walked towards her with a gentle hand but Angel disappeared in a flash like a will-o-the-wisp and soon there was no sign of her anywhere.

Meg walked slowly back to join me on the seat. We just sat there as she had suggested, trying not to think of anything in particular but my mind carried me off to the distant past. There were trees I remember, pear and apple in full bloom. And a field of spring lambs and a slow river and a bridge. I stood on the bridge and watched the dark shadows over the water. I sat down on a large stone facing the river and lifted my face to the refreshing breeze and had barely closed my eyes in rest when I heard a woman's voice. It was Nana and she was calling my name. "Kathy," she called over and over again and each time her voice seemed fainter and further away. The waters of the river reflected the green of the trees. Over our heads was the bluest sky, but the colours mingled and everything around radiated this liquid green light which surrounded me completely, so that I felt myself gradually enveloped in it. I breathed deeply to fill my lungs with this pure air.

The voice called again, "Kathy!" but it was Meg lifting me gently by the hand and telling me it was time to go in for supper.

Kathy Lavelle

Chapter 22

We had just finished supper in the kitchen and I knew that Shirley would want to talk. She said, "Please take this chair by me. I hear better from this side. You were speaking yesterday of your Nana. I dreaded the loss of my own mother, despite her advanced years. When she finally left us it took a long time to grasp that I would never see her again. It has been long in my mind to talk with someone who has lived as I have with life and death and suffering and adversity. There is a story I want to tell you and I played a part in it. There is a particular place always in my mind when it comes to this story. But I will tell you another time. Talking tires me out." That was strange indeed coming from Shirley.

"It is your gift for listening I appreciate," she said and I smiled to myself. "I started telling you about these asylums. If you think this place is bad, I can tell you, conditions were atrocious in the old days. There was no provision for cleanliness or comfort much less for anything resembling therapy. Lunatics, as they called them, were often chained and brutally treated, in the hope of driving out the devils that possessed them. The first humane lunatic asylum was founded by the Quakers, but milder treatment did not become common until later."

When I went in for my bedtime drink, Shirley had a book in front of her and was off on her history trail again, tonight it was another episode of the history of Mental Institutions. She read out a litany of offences, "Grief, love, jealousy, pride, fright, abuse, drink, family rows and disagreements over inheritance, concussions and fractures of the skull, drink and drugs, these are all a disaster for the insane. We are all tarred with the same brush. Life in the old asylums was hard. They thought that strict discipline and routine were essential for people to get better. The asylum was like a separate world and was self-sufficient. Patients would chop wood for fires, grow food, wash sheets and they even made the nurses uniforms! Those who couldn't work were marched around great yards for exercise. The wards were locked and there were high railings around the asylum so no one could escape."

"But isn't all that much the same today?" I asked her. I knew I had heard most of this before but Shirley needed to go over it all again.

"Oh no! It was much stricter. There were even look-out points built into the staircases so staff could survey the corridors and day rooms. No one was free to explore and there was no privacy. Their lives were torn asunder. This situation persisted for upward of a century until there were radical reforms."

"They saw the need to detain the furiously mad and dangerous in some secure place, a lock-up house of correction where the disturbed in mind might be herded with other disturbers of the peace. Inmates were regarded as brutes and treated with extreme cruelty. It would make your blood curdle," she said.

"There were horror stories of lunatics chained in underground dungeons, whipped and jeered at, cells where the stench made you instantly sick. Sometimes as many as sixteen women were cooped up for the day in a cell eight feet square. I can assure you the institutionalising of the mad wasn't the same as it is today. You and I wouldn't be holding a conversation like this, sitting around a table drinking tea and eating cake."

"It was a dark age, associated with vagrants, paupers, criminals and beggars. The deploying of brutality would be shocking to us, so many making a living out of torturing these poor creatures. The greatest failings of this system stemmed from a failure to attend carefully to patients needs. They were excessively cold in winter and overbearingly hot in summer, causing many of the inmates to commit suicide. The poor dears were often chained up in dark cellars, stretched on damp ground or on cold paving stones. I believe there were mountains of potatoes and bread, more than you would think the world population could consume in a hundred years but very little else to eat."

"But things have improved. Their doors and windows are open, their rooms lighter and there are long airy corridors. Their diet has become extraordinarily good and proper for them, even though I say so myself, and every week menus are viewed by a committee of governors. But you know the good thing nowadays is that here we have communal lounges where residents can watch television or attend other social events such as the country dancing we have on Saturday evenings."

Although I was sometimes tired of her ramblings, I had learned a lot from Shirley. Every day she read the newspaper right through. We often talked about the articles, and Shirley was adamant that I read the paper myself.

Meg was right. She always told me to count my blessings. I had good friends, decent food, hobbies if I wanted them and of course my books, my greatest passion at that time. My life had accelerated to a different level. Early evening sunlight streamed in through the high windows and danced across the floor all around us. I began to think that this place was not so bad after all.

Kathy Lavelle

Chapter 23

It was a lovely spring day. Something happened that was to change the course of my whole life, It was another consultation with Doctor Charles. He stood up, walked out from behind his desk and greeted me with a smile, smartly dressed in a pin-striped suit. In my mind I compared him with Doctor Mac who had an unkempt appearance, slightly unshaved and with stains all down the front of his jacket.

I wore Nana's wedding ring, the only treasure I possessed apart from the small photo on my dressing table. Charles looked up with a frown and seemed to scrutinise his notes.

"Were you married?" he asked nodding towards the ring.

"Oh no, this belonged to my Nana," I said, stroking it lovingly.

He smiled again. His approach was one of kindness and tenderness. "I'm afraid I am going to ask you the same questions which I know you have probably answered over and over again."

I nodded. "I know. It's all right."

"Take your time. Just tell me briefly why you were sent here. You don't have to tell me the whole story today. I'll be back next week."

At first I wondered if he already knew the answers, or if he thought I was truly incapable of memory or that in some sense I was actually insane. I knew it would be difficult to articulate but once I started I seemed to have the urge to go on.

My thoughts were now pouring out in sentences, as I told Charles the whole horrifying story. A vision of Johnny was before me again. The pain intensified when I described the images of those dreadful memories of what he had done, the escape across the river, rain whipping into my face, turning up my coat collar against the gusts of wind, trying to run as fast as I could away from the scene, my clothes ragged and dishevelled, fluttering in all directions.

I told him how I felt dirty and tortured with remorse and how Johnny flew into a rage and shouted in a brutal, furious way, how my anguish reached its peak when he threw me a final look filled with loathing. I swallowed with an effort to go on with my story. I described how I was able to move my body a few steps away from Johnny's eyes and his distorted face. I couldn't stop speaking. I told Charles how he took a piece of rope from his pocket and wrapped it round my neck to threaten what he would do if I told anyone, "If you go running or shouting, you're dead." I honestly believed he was capable of doing anything. I was seized with terror. I was reliving every minute of the ordeal, my eyes wide with fear and a moan of terror escaping from me.

"You don't have to go on," he said. "You are bringing back some very painful memories."

"It's all right," I said. "I want to go on."

I knew my account was disjointed but I tried my best to be as honest as I could. I just kept talking. I knew he was here to help me and I wanted him to know every detail. I told him of Johnny's mad frenzy and how I was shaking with fear at the violence and the shudders of this wild animal. I remembered how Johnny in his alarm thinking my father was coming up the hill, had quickened his steps to conceal himself in the darkness behind a boulder. I stepped back and went down the hillside, and a resounding scream escaped from me before his hand could stifle it. All this time, I was paralysed by fear and confusion. When he knew the coast was clear, he deafened me with his shouts and curses.

He said a woman is just another kind of domestic animal and must be treated like one. I was terrified. When he had finished with me he turned his eyes away from the blood-shattered ground and ran off like a madman.

My dress was soaked and cold on my skin, and Nana had helped me peel it off and get dry clothes from my small chest of drawers. I lay on the bed and curled in on myself. That was when someone outside me had cast a shadow over my whole life. By then my face was in my hands and I cried. It brought everything back to me and I was filled with fury at what he had done to me. I wanted Charles to put his arms around me and comfort me.

"I don't know what to say," Charles came forward and held my hand. "It's clear that you have been very cruelly and unjustly treated. The reason you were committed here was because of the terrible crime of your uncle. It was unlawful of Father Lynch to suggest something so terrible if he knew it to be untrue. I'm searching in my mind for an interpretation of these evil deeds. In those days, the illegitimate child was thought to carry the sin of his mother.   This was long ago in the forties and fifties but that doesn't excuse such awful treatment of innocent young girls."

Charles started chatting with me for a few minutes about nothing in particular just to put my mind at ease.   "We will stop for a break, some tea and biscuits," he looked across to Nurse Frances who pressed a bell. I had forgotten the pleasure of being spoken to kindly by a doctor. There was no one like him. I knew instinctively that he was the first medical professional who believed me and was willing to try and help me.

"There is something else I was going to tell you but I think you have had enough for one day. What I will do is arrange another appointment for you tomorrow morning. Is that okay?"

I thanked him and took solace from the warmth of his hand. This was the first time I had any real feelings for a man since arriving in that place. Johnny had given me a mistrust of men in general. I couldn't sleep. All that night I thought of what Charles had said and wondered what he was going to discuss with me at our next meeting. I dreamed he held me in his arms and I couldn't wait to meet him again.

Meg was the only one I had told about my feelings, how Charles had completely beguiled me, but she assured me it was only temporary. "We all go through these stages of infatuation. It's only a crush. No doubt every girl in this place feels exactly the same about him. And anyhow he is a happily married man with two beautiful daughters." But despite what Meg had said, I could feel the sensation rippling through me, shooting from head to toe, emanating from where his hand had touched mine.

.

Kathy Lavelle

Chapter 24

I was first on Charles' books for the following day. "I didn't want to keep you in suspense," he said as he opened the large sheaf of notes and my medical history.

"It's a bit early to say but I am willing to recommend your release. But first I would like to know how you feel about that? You have educated yourself and made a positive contribution to the life and work of this institution, almost like a member of staff. You would have no problem fitting into society."

"That scares me. It is a daunting thought. I have never had any visitors and I have no idea how things developed at home after I was taken away."

"I can appreciate how you feel. We haven't got much information either about your molester or about your parents, your Nana or your sister. But we will investigate all of this before any decisions are made and we will keep you informed at every stage of this investigation. As you can appreciate, we also have to assess you for release back into the community but I can't see any problems with that."

"I'm afraid I have to ask you again some of these wearying old questions which I'm sure you would wish we would stop asking. But I do feel there may be some gain in doing so." Charles went through his notes and confirmed some of the information previously recorded. Then he sat forward in his chair and put his hand on a newspaper. "Just yesterday I heard something that makes me feel that nothing is impossible. I thought I would tell you about Fr. Lynch."

I wanted to say, "Please don't mention that name," but I said nothing.

"Did you see it in the papers too?"

I didn't know what he meant and whatever it was, it must have escaped Shirley's attention too. I nodded and said nothing. I knew this was too sensitive an issue so I immediately wanted him to change the subject. He had hit on a delicate nerve and I needed to move on. But I said nothing because there was nothing useful I could say. Instead I started to cry inwardly.

"I have been reading through Father Lynch's declaration again and thought I would try and find if he was still alive. I don't mean to upset you but I read something in the paper about a Father Lynch. The name kept ringing in my ears and I wondered if he was the same person. You said he was a young priest probably about ten years older than yourself. That would make him about forty years old now. This seems to be the same person."

"No it wouldn't be the same man," I thought," but I suddenly sat up. Yes it was. Charles went on speaking, "I read the names of previous parishes and earlier victims. One incident would have happened the year before he put you away. One abuser protecting another, sweeping everything under the carpet. He was twenty six and newly ordained then. That was his first parish. He preached fire and brimstone and the seven deadly sins from the pulpit. In those days the priest was on a pedestal. His word was the law of the land. His decisions were the right ones and he had somehow managed to get the local doctor to accept his views. He was respected by people in high places."

Charles looked down at my file and I was shocked at this new revelation. "After all these years people are coming forward with allegations of abuse. One young woman said she had suffered years of terrifying abuse from Fr. Lynch which had cast a shadow over her life." Charles turned the newspaper over and I could see the glaring headlines with Fr. Lynch's name and photo in black and white. The VILLIAN PRIEST the press called him. I was the innocent victim of my brutal uncle and he knew it. He conspired with my father to have me sent to the asylum. It made me feel nauseated to look at his photo and the report on his crimes.

Charles read some of the article, "He sexually abused vulnerable young boys after football matches a court heard recently. One young man stated that the full horror of the abuse had caused him a mental breakdown. The governors of the school and the local bishop refused to comment."

Charles noticed that my face had gone deadly white. It seemed to me that Father Lynch had two sets of rules, one for himself and one for his congregation.

"Isn't this the same man who had you put away all those years ago?"

I was so shocked I could only nod my head in disbelief.

"I know all this information is a sensitive and worrying issue for you. However I will follow my instincts and work with the courts to bring this man to justice. No doubt other cases will come to light and what is called for is a full investigation of all his actions both before and after his ordination to the priesthood. He is a dangerous paedophile who has committed the most hideous crimes against young people and children. He pleaded not guilty to all the charges at the Crown Court but we have not heard the end of him yet. That man is not going to walk free."

I'd spent years trying to obliterate his face from my memory and I didn't want to see him now but Charles assured me that, if he could help it, I would not have to stand in court and testify against him.

He saw my distress and immediately changed the subject. "You have a sister," he said and a smile appeared on his face. "But we can't put you out on the road and say 'right off you go'. We need to make sure that people outside are prepared for your homecoming. And of course we need to know that this is what you yourself want for your future. You are certainly not mentally ill and should never have been sent here. Like many others you were a victim of a corrupt system."

I went outside the door, took off my shoes and walked along the corridor in my bare feet. Many things interrupted my thoughts. Scenes were unfolding before my eyes. Large tears sprang from my eyes. My heart pounded violently and I bowed my head dejectedly. I was trembling and anguish seemed to reveal the depths of my soul. Was it about Father Lynch or the thought of going home or was it to do with my feelings for Charles?

I went back to Shirley but I didn't have to tell her about the article. She had seen it all but had kept the papers hidden to protect me until I knew about it first. She held me against her warm body and then brought out the cake tin, her cure for all ills.

She talked about distant memories and not so distant, past and the present, ranging from precious memories to the present drama. Shirley wanted to drive out my despair and lighten my affliction but was afraid she would make things worse. Was I in fact as normal as the people we hear about outside. Was I ready for my freedom? A difficult decision lay ahead. All the while I was endeavouring to asses my situation but getting nowhere. After nearly fifteen years of my life in this place I seemed at times to be surprisingly very much at home but many questions were running through my head.

I dreamed about Charles that night. He was still speaking. Then he closed my notes and replaced them in the filing cabinet. He invited me to walk with him in the garden but it was not a garden surrounded by high walls.

Chapter 25

There was something about Nick. The way he walked, the way he talked, something in his voice that scared the life out of everyone. "He was a murderer who wandered free amongst innocent young men," Shirley told me. "This maniac murdered two of his sisters, and murdered his young wife after he had smothered their two week old baby. To think a human being could inflict such atrocious acts of violence on his own family is unbelievable.

"His anger spilled over into murder after a family row," police said. His wife had been suffering from severe post-natal depression and Nick's two teenage sisters were there to help out with the baby. I shudder even at the mention of his name. He had no idea that his wife had broken down after the birth of their baby daughter. He attempted to drown her but finally in a fit of rage killed her in such a violent way. When his sisters arrived on the bloody scene he stabbed them both to death.

"The worst part of it is that he showed no pity, no remorse, but just walked around like a zombie. At his arrest he had ranted, smashed everything in sight and grappled with police. His face is like a Halloween mask with that large scar down one side. Wardens keep a close watch on him day and night trying to rein in his violent impulses."

And the baby. I covered my ears. There was no way I wanted to hear what he had done to his little daughter. The thought of Tommy and the biscuit tin, the nightmarish brown paper package flashed before my eyes every time I saw him.

"The strange thing was that he had been treated at Broadmoor and was considered cured," Shirley went on. "Not fit to be sent back out into the community, but placed here where under close supervision and with the correct medication his behaviour could be monitored and controlled. Would you believe it?" And now Nick was looking even more notorious, with his wild eyes and ragged beard. He stood there smiling, a frantic, manic look on his face, and was beginning to look more and more like the picture of a wild-eyed madman. From the distance I found myself staring as his scar. It ran from his forehead down to his chin pulling his lip up into a hideous grin. He came at other patients wildly hurling abusive language, but the wardens were on the spot instantly to remove him. Some patients considered him a laughable affair but he terrified me.

"He won't harm anyone," Meg said. "He is on very strong medication" She led me out into the grounds and we stood looking out over the countryside. The landscape was deep and wide, and a breeze blew across it. We stood there and watched the cows and the sheep and the men with their sheep dogs. The day was warm and full of harvest smells. A golden glow was settling over the fields. The faraway fields were humming with the new combine harvesters through the ripe wheat. A lot of fields had already been harvested and the huge new-style hay bales were being loaded onto trailers and taken into the large sheds behind the buildings. It had been a bumper harvest with large potato crops, acres of peas and cabbages and turnips. The farm had now grown into a profitable business with more than enough to supply the kitchen and substantial amounts left over for the local markets.

We gazed at the cloudless sky and the yellow sun that no longer gave off any heat, and walked beneath tall, bare trees, down the paths and between old gravestones. The birds were already gathering on the tops of fences, flocking to fly south. When Meg decided to go back to her room, I moved further through the gardens.

The light had faded and as I walked along the path I constantly turned round as though expecting something to happen and became even more frightened for I could see what looked like a human shape in the night. I felt myself trembling all through. I paused for a moment, standing motionless in the dark.

I knew it was Nick following me, full of anger and hatred. I was convinced he had escaped from his cell in the men's quarters. Only on the previous day, I saw from the window, he had threatened everyone's life out there in the yard. And now he was going to carry out the threat. I was frightened and bewildered and bravely striving to hide it, trying to stay calm but it was quite plain to me I was being followed.

There was a heart-stopping cry and after it a long scream and the sound of a woman's voices moaning. There were some other strange sounds coming from inside the building but I knew there was something more sinister happening out here in the dark.

I could feel his fury, his body struggling between anger and outrage and his overwhelming need to get his revenge on the first person who crossed his path. I tried to find an escape but the dark figure stood between me and the main building. I could see the bulky shape stepping behind a tree and I tried to cry out in the night, while around me the wind shrieked and tossed like some angry monster. It was Nick without a doubt, finally out to get his revenge. My blood curdled and I could already feel the angry gleam in his eyes. I was helpless with fright, shivering with fear and cold and I huddled down and burrowed into a corner of the hedge. The steps got closer and I stood frozen on the spot. Then the face was lit up by the light on the pillar.

"Shirley," I screamed and collapsed into her arms.

"You silly girl, what are you doing out here on your own at this time of night."

Kathy Lavelle

Chapter 26

Charles reached into a filing cabinet and took out a sheaf of papers from a new folder all neat and clean, and not the old brown scruffy files which Dr. Mac had stacked up on the side of this desk.

"Nice to see you again Kathy," his voice was calm and welcoming.

"Thanks for seeing me so soon," I had found my voice and Charles had made it easy for me to relax.

"You know I meant what I said yesterday. You may rest assured that every possibility of justice has been afforded in your case. I will leave no stones unturned until I get justice for you." I was still staring at him and a strange sensation had taken possession of me. He was a strong, gentle man with kind hands. Was it possible to love a person more than oneself? Charles had brought some order to the chaos of my life, and was a ray of light shining through the darkness, but Meg was right. My feelings for him were only infatuation. He was a married man with two daughters. But he was the first medical person who had given my case any serious consideration. He was the first human being I had met in this office and I was physically attracted to him.

There was no end to the stories about Johnny. I started again and it seemed as though I would never stop. Johnny walked in one day holding up a dead rabbit in his left hand and swinging it over my head. He had it by the legs and there were spots of red on the floor. He skinned and gutted it on the kitchen table right in front of me. I tried to get out the door but he pushed me back and told me I needed to watch. He took out its red, bloody insides and dangled something gory in front of my eyes. "This is what I will do to you if you don't keep that stupid mouth shut."

"Another day he called me out to the chicken coop and made me watch as he gripped a chicken between his knees and as it struggled to get free he wrung its neck with a quick vicious movement. The chicken twitched and moved about for a while and then went still. I dreaded his presence in the house every evening and waited patiently at night for darkness and an escape into Nana's room."

"At this time I was under unbelievable pressure. Because of my pregnancy, my life had entered a vicious downhill spiral. I couldn't imagine how I was going to get through each day until the baby was born and I didn't dare think what would happen after that. I just dragged myself through each relentless day until I was banished here indefinitely to live out these recurring nightmares."

"Once he jumped down from a rock and landed at my feet. I tried to race down the hill, crashing into thorns but he grabbled at my hair as I tried to escape. The wire on the fence was mangled and torn with a great gaping hole at one end, enough for me to crawl through but my dress was in tatters. The sun had disappeared down behind the hill and I could just make out the farm from there, a tiny speck right under the horizon. I didn't know how I would ever make it. I would have to tell my mother some kind of story that would explain why my hair was in such disarray, my clothes torn, and my shoes covered in mud. But the house was quiet. It was the time of day when everyone was in the milking shed."

"I didn't know how sore I would be in the morning or how the bruises would appear along my thighs and chest, on the insides of my arms and around my neck. I thought I couldn't hide the truth. I got a basin of hot water and took a facecloth and lathered the soap and scrubbed hard with the rough towel and my skin turned red and sore. I reached for clean clothes that would cover my arms and neck. No amount of washing would take away the traces of his crime. My panic gave way to utter exhaustion and I wondered all that night and in the nightmares that followed how my life would ever be normal again. A deadly chill had crept though my body every time I saw him. He had become a barbarian."

I paused but Charles didn't interrupt.

"I developed a poor sense of myself, a miserable sense of my own worth as a person. I used to stand at the window looking out across the tangle of weeds in the back garden and my head was screaming like the rooks on the bare limbs of the trees. Nana told me to keep busy, to try and hold on to whatever little life there was left in me. Nana is everywhere in my mind. It seemed to me that she is there in the flowing of the waters in the distance and the blowing of the breeze. But my recurring nightmares bring me back to the bad times. The wind changed and carried my hope away. Now all I have is my shame and there is no more memory of bright colours lighting up the sky. I look back into the past with intense hatred and revulsion and always find that I can't fight it off."

Charles had sat and listened patiently, without taking notes. I know now that this was out of respect for all the suffering and humiliations that I had endured. He had his hands joined like he was praying.

I talked again about home, Johnny and Father Lynch. "In my mind I heard the bells ring out to call us to church. Father Lynch was preaching a passionate sermon on the transience of life compared to the eternity of God's grace and exhorting us to live each day preparing ourselves for death and the final judgement, so we must not be tempted by earthly pleasures, but be ever ready for our Saviour. He went into his glorious fire-and-brimstone sermon. Johnny sat in the front pew and nodded in agreement. At that time the whole service became meaningless to me. When the sunlight came through the stain glass window, a rainbow of colours fell directly on Nana's ring, a band of gold on her hands folded across her lap, fingering the beads she always carried."

"I believed then that she was the only one fit to face God in this eternal judgement."

Charles just sat there in silence and disbelief and he spoke softly. "Do you go to the services in the church here?"

But the services here were very different. The church was a bright, airy place, with tall stain glass windows and sunlight pouring down filling the place with light and falling across the pulpit where the vicar stood straight and strong. His sermons were sometimes on the theme of pain and accepting that life was full of it, on enduring it and on embracing the closeness to God that suffering could bring. These sermons did my heart and my soul some good. By the time the vicar climbed down from the pulpit the place was humming with godliness, real human understanding and forgiveness.

On another day the vicar told us, "Our sins aren't really sins but accidents that are set in motion by forces beyond our control. Sometimes we are here because of the sins of others." He seemed to have a great understanding of human nature and an awareness of some of the injustices surrounding his congregation. I was so relieved in spirit. It gave me a sense of wellbeing and spiritual renewal.

Charles waited until I looked up.

"You were miles away," he said. "We are going to get hold of these people and bring them to justice. You have suffered a lifetime torturing yourself. More and more of your inner life and emotions have now become a matter for medics like me and therapists. You have tried too hard to sweep these things away into some closet but they have come out at night to haunt you. You have been a victim of ruthless misinformation, falsely incarcerated here and there has previously been no intention of any kind to set you free but the courts will sit in careful judgement and I know that the outcome will be positive. Believe me!"

He talked some more and held my hand warmly before I went back to the kitchen. That was magic to me. It was a transition between my former life and what was still to come.

Chapter 27

"You'll soon be going home." Those were Charles' words at our last meeting. "There seem to be no grounds for keeping you here in perpetuity, to destroy the future of an innocent girl, but we will work for your release. You could be home before the end of the year."

But what is home? I had asked myself that question since the day it all began and that day now seemed like a lifetime ago. I asked it again and again, tumbling it over and over in my mind. In happier times home was Nana and my little sister Rosie. Home was being with Michael out there by the river, running to get out of the rain, jumping over the broad stones in the water, standing on the blue bridge watching the sunset.

The memories had faded and now home was my work in the kitchen with Shirley, my books, my evening chats with Meg in her cosy little room.   And now Charles, I didn't know where this was going, but I wasn't sure that I wanted to leave all this behind. It was now the only life I knew.

Meg had often told me to take a deep breath. "It calms the mind, gets rid of anything that isn't useful, beautiful or joyful," she said. "All that truly matters in the end is that we are loved. Get outside every day. Life isn't tied up with a pink ribbon but it's still a gift. Friends are the family that we choose for ourselves." And that summed it up. I had chosen my friends and made a new life here.

Charles' questioning was calm. His voice was gentle. His manner solicitous. He ran through a few preliminary questions and then moved on to the events of the day.

I could still remember Nana, all smiles and hugs and jokes but that was long ago and far away. I had overcome my nervousness. I remember my first consultation with Dr. Mac sitting behind his desk with his newspaper, and my short, panicky, monosyllabic replies. Something in his tone sounded bitter and I didn't know how to respond.

But now there was new life everywhere and I no longer swept the things I'd suffered under the rug. Everything was out in the open and everyone was here to help, sympathetic to my needs. This had increased my self-esteem.

In a way my life here had been a mystery. In an institution like this, many had suffered in some way at the hands of the staff but for me there was no admonishing, the way they treated the insane. "You are not mad," everyone told me. "The mad people, the evil people are out there somewhere, those who put you here." They all said the same.

"You look beautiful to me. Everything you do is of interest to me," Meg had told me.
Almost everything I know I have learned from Meg.

In the early days, I was scared of men but Shirley said I had nothing to fear. "During the day they have their own dining area and separate exercise yards. At night they keep the men locked away in a different wing of the building. In the old days they caged them like wolves when the sun went down but things have moved on."

My arms opened wide to embrace the night, and my voice started to hum a song I vaguely remembered Nana sing long ago. I talked with Meg again about my feelings for Charles, how I thought about him all the time and dreamed about him.

"We are all the same when it comes to love. Sometimes it can make fools of everyone, but I'm not saying that is true about you," she looked straight into my eyes, "Be careful you're not living an illusion. You know nothing can come of it and as I said before, probably every other patient in the building feels exactly the same about him. To you he is special and treats you as the only special person in the world. But he treats everyone else as special too. That's his job, to make patients feel understood and affirmed and to build up their self-esteem. I can see it in your eyes how you are besotted. But that happens to most of us. Just keep your feelings to yourself. Don't do or say anything foolish. It will go away. I can guarantee it will and I know what I'm talking about. It has happened to me more than once."

The next time I went into Charles' clinic I saw all the usual filing cabinets. It immediately gave me a sense of hush and history. I suspected there were some things in these cabinets that people would need lawyers to sort. There were all sorts of tiny histories and big histories locked away, notes on hundreds of patients. Charles respected everyone's history and gave everyone the same right to his understanding. He recognised that things were very different in the forties and fifties when most of us were sent here from all over the country and I knew that personally he would try to travel back in time to adequately appreciate those differences. He did what he could to help make compensations and undo hurts, but sadly and inexcusably those before him had thought it best to let them lie.

"It is all old history and what would it serve now to dig it up," was the old attitude.

But Charles wanted to dig it up. "I have been trying to assess your situation. I've been digging away at it for you, trying to get back to some of the background and I think I have come up with some interesting conclusions."

I tried to act normally but I seemed to have some difficulty in meeting his eyes. I was looking mostly at the bulk of my file on his desk. Dr. Mac used to thumb noisily through at least a dozen manila folders before he could remember which of his patients had come to see him. I'm convinced he didn't even know some of our names. He couldn't recognise us by sight. "Yes this is it," he would say his eyes wandering. "Yes then, what was your question?"

But Charles had it all prepared before I came in, the large two-sided manila folder. So much had been written about me but I don't think anyone had read it. Nothing, until now, had ever been done to fully assess my situation.

It was something about his smile, his enthusiasm and most of all his kindness that made me fall in love with Charles. I know what Meg said but an aching panic took me over and I couldn't help myself.

"Yes you will soon be going home," Charles said again. Did I want to be released? Did I want to leave Meg, and Matron and Shirley and Charles?

Kathy Lavelle

Chapter 28

I was travelling with Charles along the country lanes, but the loud gong woke me from my happy dream. I leapt out of bed, washed and dressed quickly and reported to my post in the kitchen. There was great commotion and I knew straight away there was excitement in the air. Matron, Shirley and Meg sat at the table, huddled together over something that had arrived by post the day before.

"Come and join us. We're going to be on television," Shirley waved the letter in front of my eyes.

"Well, we haven't agreed yet," Meg said. "I expect you remember those gentleman who interviewed us some time back. They are writing a new book on the history of mental institutions and want us to give them some inside information. Shirley and I go back a long way and have witnessed many changes over the years. They are beginning by making a comparative study of past and present," She seemed to be a little bit more apprehensive than Shirley. "To be honest I don't particularly fancy the idea of being on television. I think they are trying to prove that things are so good nowadays that some of us are refusing the option of freedom."

Shirley used to say when TV was first installed, "Isn't it great, all these funny people right here in your living room and you don't even have to go to the flicks anymore." But now she was gasping with surprise. "Just think, instead of just watching TV, we will actually be on TV ourselves, being watched by millions of people all over the world."

"I don't think it is that sort of programme," Meg said. "It's not 'Top of the Pops' material you know. It will probably be viewed on some obscure documentary channel, or maybe Professor Hoffman just wants to use it for training purposes. "

But Shirley had already made a huge contribution to Professor Hoffman's work. She had given a lot of answers to their questionnaires and no doubt she would be the key person in these interviews. She was the expert here. I know she had been following Professor Hoffman's studies in some magazine and had written to him on numerous occasions. She knew about this new comparative study. Ever since I arrived here, Shirley had been making these comparisons herself so who better to work on the documentary. She talked about new approaches between doctors and staff with their patients and had told us on more than one occasion how the former barbarous conditions with strait-jackets and patients chained up were an absolute disgrace.

"It's not the same anymore," she said.

"We need to call an urgent meeting with the board of governors." Matron was already leaving to make some phone calls.

The following week we all worked flat out in the kitchen preparing a lavish meal for the Board of Governors. Shirley was preparing the dishes she knew were favourites amongst them.

They ate in the board room. This was a committee of prominent local men including gentry, aristocrats, magistrates and the local Vicar. It was their job to ensure that the place was run effectively and efficiently. Their annual report provided a wealth of statistical rankings such as the causes of illnesses or the number of patients working in various parts of the asylum and the value of the farm and gardens.

The boardroom table was set for twelve, with a white damask linen table cloth, silver candelabra and a huge vase of flowers as a centrepiece. Matron always attended these Board meetings but on this occasion Shirley, Meg and I had been invited as well. The meal was an informal affair with introductions and friendly chat around the table. When the last course had been served and everyone had complimented Shirley and her staff, the formal part of the proceedings began.

The chairman reached down for his note pad. "Well who is going to be the first to kick off?"

"I think we owe that honour to Shirley," Matron smiled across the table to where Shirley sat now blushing from all the compliments. "After all she is the one who seems to have instigated this whole affair. I believe she knows Professor Hoffman personally."

"I have never actually met him but we have communicated in writing on several occasions and I think we are on the same wavelength." She filled everyone in on the nature of Professor Hoffman's study and the reason why he wanted to come and visit 'The Manor'. "I will tell the professor how institutions like ours have become more cheerful, busy, orderly societies where there is gardening, walking, drawing, music and a variety of manual occupations. I hope to be able to make a contribution to a desperately needed new history of asylums or mental hospitals as they are now called. I can bring some of the areas of ignorance more sharply into focus. This approach must be open-minded, a true record of what is happening today. I have written a lot on the subject myself and tried to avoid looking at my sources through psychiatrists' eyes but rather to focus on what is actually happening all around us. For too long psychiatrists have been passing clinical judgements on who was truly sane or mad. I have quite a lot to say about some of these mad old doctors. I have made the use of quotations and looked at what brought about changes in our institutions like political pressures, reorientation of religious people and new training methods. For a long time nobody investigated insanity or advanced its treatment. There was a wealth of assumptions about madness in circulation among secular culture high and low but research has remained patchy, up till now that is. Let's hope that Professor Hoffman's study will change all that."

We just sat is awe listening to Shirley. "You could be a professor yourself," the Chairman said looking across at Shirley and smiling at all the distinguished guests. She blushed again as everyone looked at her in admiration.

Then Matron was invited to speak. "We are all pioneers of humane treatment where patients are now encouraged to use self-restraint in their behaviour. I would like to think that we now use an approach with kindness, and with restraining only where absolutely necessary. The new idea is to integrate patients into family domestic activities and encourage them to work and take exercise, and become engaged in various sports. Physical exertion while working and exercising in the grounds tires patients and gets rid of excess energy so that they are less disruptive and it supposedly diverts their minds from irrational thoughts. Our buildings here are secluded in the countryside behind walls and hedges and set in parks surrounded by a belt of trees with views down to the harbour, to ensure the patients have peace and quiet. Fortunately we are now aware of the benefits of treating patients without mechanical restraints such as chains and straitjackets. Our regular inspections, as you know, are important to make sure we are avoiding any malpractice. Detailed medical statements are examined frequently and Medical officers visit the wards unexpectedly by day and night."

Meg sat patiently waiting her turn to speak. "We must be proud of the fact that the staff here are a close-knit family, even sharing some of the facilities with the patients. Many of our staff were out there playing cricket last Sunday. Others were singing in the choir or playing in the band or performing in our small theatre to provide important light relief for patients and staff. The post-war era brought about more liberal ideas and now drugs bring more effective relief and enable greater control of patients' conditions without physical isolation. There is much greater freedom of movement provided for patients with less locking of ward doors. But I think we have a long way to go on many of these issues. An Important part of our job is helping patients speak, communicating their thoughts. We must try to get inside their heads, to know how they regard themselves. But finally I must say there is a great deal of kindness in this place and as we all know kindness is usually met by kindness."

I sat there nervously, hoping I might be able to make some small contribution to the study. "I agree with everything that had been said already and in my opinion, Doctor Charles has made enormous changes with his approach. When I first arrived here in 1952 I was too scared to express my feelings. But Doctor Charles is a good listener. He has carefully examined all the documents and all he wants is justice for his patients. In my case, he has delved deeply into my background to find the real reasons for my being here. He has gone to great lengths with his investigation and discovered that great injustice has been done in my case and now he is working towards my release."

"Thank you Kathy," the chairman smiled down to the bottom of the table where I sat there nervously with my hands folded on my lap. It was a great relief that they didn't ask me any questions.

The chairman then went around the table and allowed each member of the board to share their thoughts on the forthcoming TV broadcast. "Now does anyone want to add anything to what they have already said?"

"They will examine everything," Shirley wanted to talk about her own area of expertise. They will look at the layout of the kitchen, how food is stored, standards of hygiene, the new washing machines. We have so much to be proud of. I just can't wait to show it to the whole world."

"I don't think we have any problems in that area," the chairman looked appreciatively in Shirley's direction. Now I will invite my colleagues on the Board to ask any questions from the speakers.

Finally the chairman said they would have to convene another meeting for the following week, and invite some of the staff who held the most prominent positions including the head gardener, the lodge porter, heads of the various workshops, sports trainers and anyone else he thought would be part of the study and who might possibly be interviewed by Professor Hoffman's team.

We breathed a sigh of relief when the last of the visitors had left the building and we made a beeline back to the kitchen. Shirley put the kettle on and switched on the radio. The Beatles sang, 'She Loves You'. Shirley was on a high. "She Loves you Yea Yea Yea. What sort of a song is that?" she said waltzing around the kitchen and reaching up for the cake tin.

"Television hasn't half brought us back in touch with reality and brought us up to date in the world out there. And now bringing the world in here," she laughed.

Kathy Lavelle

Chapter 29

Shortly after the board meeting, I was transferred to administrative duties although I still maintained close links with the kitchen. My work did not start until eight o'clock in the morning but I was always up at five so that I would have time to go into the kitchen for an early breakfast and to lend a hand. I had become a sort of private secretary to Matron. My new responsibilities included answering the phone, writing letters and very often just sitting there talking things through with Matron. Hers was a lonely job which required a lot of discretion in dealing with things of a very confidential and sometimes very delicate nature.

But my cosy little chats with Meg were still the highlight of my day. She congratulated me on my new role and continued to give me advice. I liked that.

"Nobody owns your mind," she told me, "or your faculties for seeing and hearing and if you are going to form judgement let them be well informed judgements but very often you will have to keep your opinions to yourself. You know that is one of the main reasons why you got this promotion. Matron appreciated your discretion. Well done Kathy. You always see the needs of others before yourself. For what are we born if not to aid one another? You are sound enough now, no need for psychiatrists."

Meg had been a teacher and she controlled people, using entreaty, humour, and tenderness. That was the only type of discipline she employed with the children she taught in her previous life and with the patients here. I witnessed the effect this had on people and the success in Meg's life, making her everyone's best friend. I realised now how much she resembled Nana whose life was always filled with love and delight despite her hardships. Nana's spirit soared over all.

I was so lucky. My life was not over. My life had just begun. And most of all there was Charles. Do you know what it is to love someone? Love had made me a different person. It had made the world beautiful again. Meg told me my eyes sparkled in the sunshine with a strange new brilliance that radiated life, vitality, warmth and beauty. I had new surging emotions and feelings that I had never had before.

I looked across at the farmyard and the arrival of the threshing machine filled me with nostalgia. I found myself staring off at the fields but I was not there. I was back on the farm. The only mechanised vehicle to come to our farm was the steam engine of the threshing machine in the autumn. In those days the sense of community was strong and threshing was a co-operative task. Men from neighbourhood farms followed the threshing machine and arrived with their pitchforks. We heard the hum of the thresher and counted the days until it would pull into our yard. Living still in the age of the horse, anything motorised that moved on wheels on the farm was to us a kind of miracle. After breakfast the engine was coaxed into life sending up smoke signals. It was one of the most sociable days of the year. As they worked, the men discussed currents events and Michael's father kept them amused with his jokes. All that day the thresher droned and the men worked steadily. There was an air of good fellowship and fun both in the farm and around the kitchen table afterwards. The men climbed up on top of the stacks of corn and fed the sheaves to the thresher and the rich coloured grain and chaff spouted out at the other end. Like a squirrel they gathered in their stores for the winter, and if the snow came heavy and they were cut off from the outside world, they were safe and self-sufficient. Facing into the winter the entire work of the farm wound down and they looked forward to the long, leisurely nights around the fire.

After the threshing, they all came into the house where Nana had prepared a big meal assisted by my mother and Aunt Jean. Few people had a wireless but my father got one and Nana enjoyed singing all the latest songs. I sat in my usual position, turning the wheel on the bellows. There was no running water or electricity and my wonderful Aunt Jean had to walk down a steep slope to the nearest well and carry the heavy buckets of water back up the slippery bank. Rosie and I used to go and help her but carrying a pail of water was heavy work. Nana must have had her own problems and concerns like everyone else but she was always cheerful. She has a knack for dealing with different people and had a good memory for names. I remembered the infectious nature of her smile and the way she managed to make everyone feel special.

I wandered over to the farmyard with Meg by my side and briefly watched the threshing machine and the memories it brought were happy ones but tinged with great sadness. Meg was also damaged by her past and by her wartime experience. She was sometimes demented by sorrow and regret. I could see a far-away look in her eyes.

"Let's go for a little walk," I said linking her arm.

She smiled at me gently. "How are you," she asked. Meg knew that I was back there where it all began. "It's good to talk," she said.

"I thought the nightmares were over but last night I was pulling a jumper over my head to hide the scars. He had reached out and grabbed the end of my long hair and yanked it hard and brought me down onto my knees in front of him. He pulled me to the ground and sat on my chest. I was begging, imploring him to stop but here is where he wrapped his hands around my neck and began to squeeze." I put my hand up to my neck.

"Nana gave me one of her pills. "It will help you sleep," she said. "It will make you calm."
"Those were dark days. It was difficult to look back on the joys of those days before. There was darkness in our world and then again I was looking for my Nana in these memories and I couldn't find her. She had simply disappeared. But then again in my grief-torn imagination Nana's spirit had become a dove, a bird that remained in my mind as one of special grace. The moment it was dark I became bitterly cold but the turf fire warmed our little house cosily. The wind stopped as suddenly as it had begun but the day had lost part of its brightness. A moon was guiding me on. I nearly tripped over a stub of rock jutting out of the ground, stumbling forward until I righted myself. A mighty thickness of heather and bracken and jutting rocks and my dreams had become such a jumble."

"Shh, there there," Meg said holding me to the warmth of her body. "You still need to let it all come out."

Kathy Lavelle

Chapter 30

It was getting late. "Well that will do for today," Meg said. Since taking up my duties as Matron's secretary, we found I had a lot more spare time to pursue my reading habits and there was still so much that Meg wanted to teach me although she had now become ill and quite frail.

We went down to the Library. Everything was sparkling new, bright curtains and carpets and rows of beautiful book shelves made by Henry and his team in the workshop. I ran my fingers along the rows of books and then moved to the next shelf, from one spine to the next, pacing the whole room. In the early days I had felt completely useless, unattractive, and worthless but thanks to Meg I had become more or less a success in the different things I had attempted. I had become more confident and I was learning to meet some of the hardest challenges head-on.

We kept up the ritual of reading aloud and I became absorbed in the unfolding of the stories which took me into dazzling journeys around the world, entering castles and caves. We took the long journeys together and read 'War and Peace' although I have to admit Meg did most of the reading but she stopped occasionally to let me read a page or two. We talked about it all the time and I was surprised to find out that when we discussed things in the kitchen, Shirley had read quite a few novels herself and always encouraged us to discuss the books we were reading.

Then we started to read poetry. I learned many of the poems by heart and I can still recite them today. Then Meg taught me to read experimental literature, modernist texts by Joyce and Woolf. To begin with I did not recognize the stories or like any of the characters but Meg had helped me understand most of them. However I knew I still had a long way to go. Finally I had begun to read everything I could lay my hands on. I thought of those time-travel stories, the ones where you go back and change one thing then everything else changes, like a ripple effect. "Oh if only it could be like that in real life!" I thought.

We discussed poetry or politics in the long winter evenings, or over the breakfast in the steamed-up kitchen but somewhere underneath a part of me remained fearful of the world outside.

Then Meg told me to watch people and how they were changing and how so many of their mannerisms and even accents were copied from the television. I began to notice all kinds of other things they had taken from TV programmes, the way they gestured to each other or sat together, even the way they argued and stormed out of rooms, like they had seen on the screen.

It was amazing really how time seemed to melt away in the company of Shakespeare and Dickens, Mark Twain and Kipling. Meg introduced me to some wonderful passages of prose and poetry, and the plays of Tennessee Williams and Arthur Miller. They were all there on the new shelves. Amongst my favourites were the works of Graham Green which Matron had collected for me at the local fairs or Church jumble sales. Meg taught me about the beauty of language, figures of speech and how a piece of writing can be enhanced.

Late one evening I looked for some bedtime reading. I picked up "The Grapes of Wrath." Steinbeck always had a way of transporting me back into the countryside where I was born.

I slept the deep sleep of nervous exhaustion. I dreamed of a baby in the room. I held Tommy in my arms in the good old days and sang him to sleep. We were having tea in the hay field. As the meadows ripened to a honey coloured hue in the sun, one of the seasonal jobs was helping to save the hay. In those days, manual labour on the land had changed little from the methods used for centuries. The hay season was one of my favourite times of the year. The men used their sharpening stones to hone the blade of the scythes, to prepare the edges of the field in preparation for the mower and then tackled the shire horse to the mowing machine when it was time for hay-making which began on a mellow summer's day. A few days later, when the swathes had dried, they moved in again, this time with pitchforks or with their hands, turning the hay so that the underside could dry. Reaping the corn took place at the end of summer when we walked alongside the ripened crops and the old reaping machine gave off a plaintive whine which carried across the heather and told of busy times. Nana Sang softly to me as she helped bind up the corn into sheaves.

Good weather was essential. Seeing a ripe field of oats with the sunlight glinting on the grain gladdened the farmer's heart but caused many a worry too until it was safely harvested. A day in the meadow was sunshine and sweat, hard work and happiness. I went with Nana as she carried home-made bread, cheese and cans of tea to the workers in the fields. They sat in a shady corner under a tree and ate their sandwiches and drank their tea from the enamel mugs, while the horses also relaxed and sampled some freshly cut hay, flicking their long tails to keep the flies at bay. It was also a time of great laughter as Michael's father told funny stories and riddles and played tricks on the children. I often walked with Nana in the dusk standing by the gap of a field counting the stacks of hay with the satisfaction of a job well done. After the work in the meadow was finished the hay was drawn home by horse and float or donkey and cart. Now the barn was full of soft golden hay, and the animals were safe against the ravages of winter no matter how harsh it might come. Larks were singing their evening choruses and we wandered through meadows bordered by complete hedges of fuchsia and honeysuckle which sent out a soft, wild, perfume mingled with the smell of new mown hay.

We sat there quietly watching the shadows fall over the darkening fields. The sun has already set but I did not draw the curtain. Twilight seeped into the room and I was almost drifting off to sleep. We had all the freedom in the world. There was endless sunshine and the world lay green and billowy beneath a brilliant, permanent blue sky. The farmyard was a depiction of colour and sound. There were horses, donkeys, cattle, pigs, turkeys, chickens and guinea pigs. Rosie and I watched Nana milk the cows. She sang as she worked, now and again squirting the milk at us. It was all so wonderful, the wide fields, and moorland, hills and valleys. No words can describe the freedom and amazement and pleasure as we ran through the fields and through the heath and heather. During that time I had a wonderful relationship with Nana. We were always seen smiling, joking and working together, but there were tears too as we shared the sadness of our lives.

There was a basic harmony between Nana and the countryside. She recognised the beauty of the earth and loved working on a daily basis. Farmers used to drive their herds of cattle to the fields and even killed their own pigs, hung them up and made bladder footballs for the children. On those distant days, we played out on the hillside until the moon came up and Nana pulled the oil lamp down from the ceiling. She taught us to shake hands and bury all our grievances as the sun went down and told us "Never let the sun go down on your wrath." We sat on the settle filled with chaff from the threshing and covered with flower bags bleached and boiled. Much of my outlook on life and many of my decisions and judgements of what is right and what is wrong, were influenced by Nana and her thoughts and philosophies.

I remembered everything. I saw myself at fourteen walking, head held high, not afraid of anything. And then I was thrust into in that measureless ocean of tears and blood.

Chapter 31

The day smelled of summer. The house and the job and the grief would all shrink to a point behind me. For some reason, I was on top of the world. The weather was beautiful. The sun was hot and the air was buzzing with bees and the scent of flowers was everywhere. The whole place was now in shadow and sunshine for summer had arrived and the chestnut tree outside was heavy with foliage. It was July. It was a warm evening at the end of a sultry summer's day and one I still remember vividly.

I strolled in to see Henry in his workshop. I had done a little woodwork with him before, in the evenings after I had finished my duties in the kitchen, only to make a couple of trays for Shirley and a little bookshelf for Meg's room.

"Oh, the very person I was thinking of," Henry said. "I am going to do a session on guitar making.

"Oh no, you weren't thinking of me? I only do basic things," I objected. "I wouldn't know where to begin."

"Ah, but that's where you are wrong. It's a session for beginners. You only need very basic skills, under the guidance of a skilled tutor," he laughed. "The course starts in the autumn. I know you don't want to be stuck down here in the long summer evenings."

It was then that I realised he wouldn't take no for an answer. In fact I even began to feel excited, not a bad way to escape the long winter nights. I began to dream about the finished product. I could hear myself boasting, 'I made this myself you know', as I strummed on my own guitar and Shirley sang along. I already knew how to play a few chords which I had learned from Meg, enough to accompany a song or two. But I knew I had to be a bit more discreet about it. Henry had told me that this was a select group of only four people. He chose people who could already play a little music. Henry always ran small workshops for safety reasons. I decided to keep quiet about the whole thing, for inwardly I knew it would probably result in a disaster for me with Henry doing most of the work.

"Oh OK, I'll give it a go" I felt that it would be no harm to try it out and I knew Henry was going to be there to bail me out if necessary. No one was going to put a gun to my head if it became impossible.

The summer flew by and on the first night of my guitar-making course I went into the kitchen in an old leather apron. Shirley had been in on the secret and exploded in convulsions of laughter. She hopped around the floor on one leg, strumming an imaginary guitar, singing, "We all live in a Yellow Submarine."

"No seriously I think it's a great idea. Good luck love," she said. "I know you can do it. You always succeed at anything you put your mind to."

"I'm not so sure this time Shirley. Maybe I have bitten off more than I can chew."

She laid a reassuring hand on my shoulder. "You'll be fine. Come in later for a cup of tea. Tell Henry to come too. You know something? I used to have a crush on Henry. But nobody has ever had a crush on me. Maybe if I had lost a bit of weight. Ah well. It's too late now."
"We all love you Shirley and you have more friends here than anybody else. The place just wouldn't be the same without you."

"Thanks love. And yes I am grateful. I wouldn't change my life for anything."

The big day arrived. The smell of fresh wood shavings greeted me at the door. Henry welcomed his new class of four expectant world famous guitar makers. This was my first attempt at anything so adventurous. Henry gave us the usual talk on health and safety and putting everything back in the right places when we had finished. Dangerous instruments were always counted after use and kept in locked cabinets. These could be lethal in a place like this.

Finally the moment arrived for the choice of woods for our guitars. I can still feel the smooth texture of the rosewood. I had quite literally never held a piece of wood like this in my life. Henry stroked a beautiful piece of workmanship, one of his own finished masterpieces. He ran his hands down the glossy sides of the guitar and murmured something about the smooth curves of the body. We were holding flat pieces of wood in our hands and I wondered how it would ever reach that shape. It was truly a magnificent sight and my vanity returned.

"Wait till one of these is my own creation," I dreamed but I had now become quite apprehensive. I knew it seemed an almost impossible task. And I wasn't far wrong. It was about the seventh night of our endeavour that disaster struck. Wood had been duly selected for the sides of the guitars and we were instructed to plane these until almost wafer thin. Henry held a finished rib up to the light and it was as sheer as gossamer. With a little effort on my part and a lot of help from Henry I would achieve my goal. I planed the rosewood so carefully back and forth and the floor was covered in wood shavings. By holding the strips up to the light I could literally see through the wood.

Now for the exciting bit! The next evening it was a matter of bending the side strips to fit neatly around the front and back sections. This was the technique, which enthralled me most. The strips were kept dampened and carefully manipulated over a hot roller. Henry guided my hands gently to get me started and showed me how to manoeuvre the curves. Then he moved around assisting the others.

I was alone impatient to see the finished result. Snap! My rib cracked. The sides of my beautiful new guitar were smashed beyond redemption. In my over-enthusiasm, I had not dampened the wood sufficiently. The other students, Max, Len and George were carefully damping and bending, damping and bending, easing the wood carefully, working slowly and meticulously. There were no short cuts. Henry was helping Max who was working quietly on the next bench when he suddenly noticed my catastrophe.

"My guitar is ruined," I cried. "I can't do this," I said in total despair. "I'm not staying here." Fighting back the tears, I rushed from the room. There was no way I wanted to see this thing again. My guitar in splinters, my dreams shattered. I wandered around a quiet spot in the garden until I had composed myself and dried my tears.

"You're back early." Shirley sensed there was something wrong when I went back into the kitchen. I was still wondering why I had attempted something so difficult.

At the end of the session, Henry came to the kitchen door and Shirley beckoned him in. "It's all right," he said with a gentle arm around my shoulders. This brought back more floods of tears.

"We've mended it. You can come back in and have a look."

I stared in disbelief. The invisible mending on my ribs was amazing. Henry had carefully glued the splintered edges together and held them in a clamp until the rib was complete.

"It's no problem," he assured me. "It happens all the time." Taking more care after this, I spent a few more weeks finishing the task.

"Cheers!" Henry produced a bottle of wine from his locker and toasted the new guitars. We laughed and drank a toast to the finished masterpieces.

I was proud of my endeavours but my pride had taken a well-deserved knock. The broken ribs are long forgotten but I have always remembered Meg's favourite saying,.

"Never give up. We were born to succeed, not to fail."

Chapter 32

A cold shiver like the shiver of death goes through my body even to think about it. I hesitate even to write about this, it is so horrible.

One morning after father had gone to the village to fetch supplies, Johnny walked in unannounced. He never knocked. It was as though the place belonged to him. His mouth curled into the evil smile which I was beginning to know only too well. Mother passed him a beer and he raised his tankard in a mocking salute and a mouthful of filthy jokes. Mother laughed at his vulgarity. Johnny gave me a smirk but I continued to look straight at him without blinking. I knew I hated him as only a slave can hate his master. All my life I was looking for something that would fill me with pride, something that would make me hold my head high but he had destroyed all that. I hated his crude stories and cruel jokes and the way he looked at me with contempt.

"You go out and chop some wood for the fire," mother nudged me off my seat.

I went over to the byre and had a chat with Nana who was still finishing off the milking. Rosie sat on a small stool beside her. I told Nana that Johnny had arrived and she just rolled her eyes up to heaven. I picked up the hatchet and went round the back but there was a cold wind whipping up and I rushed back into the house for a jacket.

The kitchen was empty. I heard noises coming from my parents' room. This room was the inner sanctuary of my parents' relationship. It had always been a place of mystery and trepidation and we had never been allowed to go in there. It was the same grunting noises I had heard on the hillside and sounds of mother giggling. I stood there glued to the spot, unable to believe what I knew was happening in the bedroom. I rushed out the door, picked up the hatchet and felt that every blow was for Johnny and now for mother. One for Johnny. One for mother. I know now why she laughed at his crude jokes, why he always had to have the best seat in front of the fire.

"How can I tell anyone, no one would ever believe me," I thought. But I did tell Nana. "It happened before to your aunt Jean," she said. Just then my father walked in the door and she clammed up. Later in our little bedroom Nana told me, "Jean was just your age.

She was pregnant and her parents forced her to marry him. She has led a life of hell."

This was the day before I witnessed the arrival of the great blizzard. It raged for two nights and two days, the snow so thick and wind-driven that in daylight it was hard to see even to the other side of the field. The universe shone with such brilliance and other glittering worlds were dotted through space. The whole world was blanketed in snow and the Aurora Borealis gave off a magical glow. For us children it was a magical time but for grownups life was at a standstill. My father was just a body on the sofa and didn't do anything around the house. In normal times he worked hard on the farm so mother always excused him and had frequently tried to make up for his shortcomings.

My nightmares increased. "If you tell anyone you'll get taken into care and you'll never see your parents or Nana or Rosie ever again," No one would believe me anyway. Then things got much worse. Get off I screamed but my screams were lost in the wind and the wildness of the place. I felt as though I was surrounded by monsters. I could tell no one for no one would believe me. Everyone seemed to take my silence as an admission of guilt. I stared at the angry rush of water over the rocks and into the fast-flowing river. I think at this impossible distance that he wanted to kill me. I seemed to have found my murderer. He gripped my neck with his ugly hands and I was choking for breath. "You were wise to keep your mouth shut to save your own skin," he growled. I could feel fear creeping through my whole body. I did not know what destiny lay in store for me. Then a tense silence came over my dream like that of children in the dark who hear footsteps they think are those prowling around outside.

The Baby In The Biscuit Tin

It makes me a little dizzy to contemplate the possibility that everything Dr. Mac told me was right. He told me my memories were distorted. But all I have left are my memories. I am not so sure this is always a good thing. I am trying to be faithful to what is in my head. Memories are dancing around and can't be controlled. He told me that memories are unreliable. But everything is always there, still unfolding, still happening in my dreams and nightmares.

I would like to think that some of my memories are not real because of Tommy and the horror of the biscuit tin, the parcel wrapped up in brown paper and travelling across the scrubby fields and the wastelands to the back of the cemetery. I am calling and calling as they lower him into the grave.

My story is stranger than fiction, full of monstrosities and horror, things I didn't want to have to say and things I didn't want to have to believe. Tommy's little garden is a refuge for birds and insects. The trees are heavy with fruit but not ripe yet. There is bindweed in the flower-beds and wild flowers in the nature area.

I must admit there are memories in my head that are curious even to me, blurred like a mist across these hills in early morning, the contents jumbled about from neglect but also from too much haphazard searching in them, like throwing things away that don't belong here, like a spring-cleaning of the mind.

Kathy Lavelle

Chapter 33

With so much extra time on my hands, I became lost in my reading with Shakespeare and Tennyson, books on American literature and volumes of history and travel books. I couldn't see much sense in reading the travel books but Meg had said, "Read everything!"

The old neglected library had now become my haven. I thought back to the early days when the shelves were falling to pieces, and books were covered in a thick layer of dust. I used to wipe off the dust with a yellow cloth, sit on a broken chair under the light of a feeble lamp and read. But now there was an enormous sofa. I curled myself comfortably and began to read but sometimes I could not take in a single word and had to go back and reread several pages or even chapters. I ran through the fountains of books to try and increase my vocabulary. And at night-time I curled up on my narrow bed, a blanket draped across my feet reading and dozing and thinking, and by the time I went to sleep I felt much restored.

I developed an even greater love of books and with every book I learned something new, about history, about people, about the world and about love. There were so many great literary works, profound and moving pieces of writing. Meg used to come into my room, the books spilling from under her arm, books of mystery, murder and mayhem and adventures of smugglers. I picked out my favourite authors and poets and travelled to grand and fearsome places, all without leaving the couch just like countless other readers had taken the journeys before me. I was amazed by how much confidence Meg had given me. Even after I had mastered the elements of reading, we kept up our ritual of reading aloud, Meg continuing reading to me to nurture my love for books. My days were simple, rising at dawn, spending the first hours in Matron's office, a break for lunch, then my walks and my reading.

In our new library, every wall was lined with shelves all the way to the ceiling. Meg was enchanting and she enchanted me. Together we had reached a new and brighter dawn. Meg said, "Now you have learned your way around sentences. You know what to do with the twenty six letters of the alphabet. There is nothing stopping you from finishing your story."

But what were such skills when I remained enslaved and why would I want to write about it? Sometimes I was lost in my reading and then there were times I was tired of being powerless. Every time I thought I saw light at the end of the tunnel, things went wrong and I was back there in the darkness.

Sometimes I needed the company of other people. "It is not good to spend too much time alone," Meg had warned me." On Saturday nights I liked to go into the large lounge where romantic music played with people slowly circling the room in a stately waltz and in another room groups gathered around the gramophone to a joyous old-time sing-along, some with eyes that were clouding with nostalgia. During the week I wandered into some of the workshops, classes on raffia or weaving I was not completely out of the woods and there were still fits of the old anxiety and inner struggles, but at other times there were feelings of peace and deep contentment that spread over me. All around the horizon were pale, fleecy clouds, never changing, never moving, like a silver setting in the flawless blue sky and a bird hopping lightly in the quiet garden, or sunlight spilling into my quiet room. But I still felt a turmoil of conflicting emotions.

Chapter 34

I went into Meg's room one morning to make her a drink. It was around ten o'clock but she was still very tired. Despite the sleeping draughts the nurses had given her, she was awake most of the night, I could see the rise and fall of pain through her frail body. She was weak like a newborn baby. Her life had now gone full circle and a wild feeling of panic and loss poured into me. I just sat there gently holding her hand. Her eyes had an unhappy burning look that I had noticed before.

And I recall one particular evening when she called for me after tea time. "Let's go out in the fresh air and get a little exercise," she said.

She had become more ill but despite the nurses' protestations, she made her way back into the gardens which had always been her haven where she could be found sitting in the herb plot which she still tried to tend, her face tilted up to the late afternoon rays of the sun, but the disease had eaten so deeply inside her and the pain was so evident. Her unruly hair flowed loose and blazed out like a grey halo around her head.

She offered her hand and I took it. I got the feeling that Meg was now beginning to lean on me. Sometimes she looked tired and weary. This wasn't like Meg. Her face was mild and her voice soft with weariness. She was still trying to help everyone but she had become weaker every day. "You must be brave," she told me and I think she was trying to prepare me for her death. I was surprised at how small her voice sounded.

"The daffodils are nearly out," she said in a whisper. "I hope I live to see the daffodils once more before I die." She wanted us all to know she was ready to pass on and that she was not scared of death.

"I'll be back with baby Anna, and Richard ....and Tommy" she looked at me for a reaction and smiled a sort of faraway smile. "And no one will ever be able to separate us again." I envied her faith. She really believed in an afterlife where we would meet all our loved ones again.

Meg tried to pull a weed from Tommy's little garden but the effort was too much for her. Only the week before, she had made a sign for Anna's plot. It was whittled from a piece of wood and hand painted in pink with little birds flying around Anna's name. This little garden was no longer a secret place. John the gardener had helped work with us on the two little plots, helped us to propagate plants and take cuttings. He stored these in one of his greenhouses. He always liked to come out and surprise us with some beautiful array of colourful plants.

Meg and I liked to sit when the weather was a little warmer. I had made a bench in Henry's woodwork class, a double bench with a small T and a small A for Tommy and Anna, carved into the wood almost invisible except to us. The beds of well prepared plants and flowers were now trying to bud with bamboos holding everything against the wind.

When the quality of aloneness settles down past, present, and future all flow together. "The greatest virtue is silence," Meg had often told me. "People can say things in the heat of the moment, sometimes irreparable things, which they later regret." I have been here a long time and have learned the virtue of silence certainly. Everybody says my little flower bed is beautiful but I don't tell them what it is, it doesn't look like a memorial. There is a small rabbit I carved in woodwork classes and lots of seasonal flowers. Today there are snowdrops, myriad of little white heads peeping through the frosty ground.

Meg could only walk slowly now leaning on my arm. The wind was in my ears and blowing my hair in my face. Meg pulled her scarf tightly around her neck. I began to think fresh air was the only thing that kept her alive as the illness ran through her body, and through her bones. "Are you all right," I asked, noticing the expression on her face and the tremor in her voice and the way she held me painfully tight as the wind blew wild in the bleak mid-February.

Meg had made a little bird table some time ago and it stood proudly over Anna's plot attracting the blue tits, the green tits, robins and sparrows and all the hungry little finches. The flowerbeds were awash with new buds. Old men with hoes were helping John with the last few weeds to make way for the abundant spring growth that always made Meg proud to be alive. Half way down the path I could see that she was about to collapse.

"The daffodils are going to be early this year," John said and walked about whistling.

"We will soon see their mighty heads swaying in the breeze," I told Meg but I don't think she heard us.

"Let's get back into the warmth of the kitchen," I said and Meg didn't object. I took her arm back towards the building. There was no hurry, as her arthritic joints let her move only in slow motion. She watched people come and go and tried to make a feeble nod at one or two she thought she recognised. She sat in her usual corner in the kitchen and I wrapped her gently in a blanket and helped Shirley prepare the hot drinks.

After I had helped Meg into bed, I went back into my own room and tried to continue with my writing. I sat staring at the pen in my hand. At first my hand was much less steady and my clumsiness made me despair at times, but little by little my confidence grew enough so that by the time I had finished I wanted immediately to start again. Sleep would not come to me. I put down my writing and returned to my books, gathering information at a ferocious rate, absorbing books like 'Madame Bovary', 'Jude the Obscure', and 'A Passage to India' until my head was giddy and the words seemed to swim and swirl in front of my eyes

Over the next few weeks most of the thaw moved across the gardens and up the hillside, field by field, warming the air and waking the squirrels from their long slumber. Spring burst out everywhere. All manner of creatures were waking up, the birds, swallows, great flocks of them flying back from Africa or some other warmer country. Perfume was rising, very delicately like a distant memory.

Kathy Lavelle

Chapter 35

I was sitting at Matron's desk with a stack of papers in front of me and for the first time in my life I did not yearn for my freedom. The wind moved a draught through the small window and I didn't want to get stuck in the past. I went over to the kitchen and put the kettle on for tea, set out cups and saucers for Shirley and myself. We just sat there quietly talking about Meg.

I was stirring memories I would rather try to forget but luckily something always seemed to turn up to keep my mind occupied and I could feel happy again, lost in my work, and forgetting everything for an hour or two. In the afternoon, I went back to the infirmary to visit Meg. She lay there staring out the window. I sponged her forehead and began to read to her but she seemed to have lost track of her story.

It was so different from the days she used to read to me, always encouraging me, especially when I was struggling through 'War and Peace'. We had been in each other company constantly since setting up the library and had been confiding in each other more than ever. Everything we told each other during these moments would be treated with careful respect. I had felt comforted and protected but now the scene was reversed. I so much wanted to do the comforting but it was not easy, watching her lie there, my beautiful heroine, now scarcely able to eat or speak. The windows were open and the breeze that fluttered through the half-drawn curtains carried the scent of lavender from the front garden.

Lying in my own little bed in the stillness of the night, I did my best to read to take my mind off my sadness but while my eyes moved across the lines of print, I listened to the night. On the edge of sleep a new sound jerked me awake, the sound of a baby, getting nearer and nearer. Tommy always came back to comfort me. Sometimes I wonder what sort of person I would have become if history had not taken such an abnormal turn and if I had grown up in the other world.

The last time I saw Johnny, I realised this could be a reason for him to kill me. My hair was matted with leaves. My clothes were in a mess. My eyes were glazed. Nana was kneeling by her bed but jumped up holding the door open.

"Kathy," she said. I heard Nana's voice. It was soft and far away. She took my hand and I squeezed it hard. I cried more and my face was mottled and swollen. I was certain the pregnancy would destroy me, would destroy my family. I could only focus on the next minute and with each minute it would get better, that slowly all of this might go away.

Nana made me a hot drink and I settled into the chair by the fire and let my body go to rest.
But I knew the sound. It was his boots on the path. And I straightened up. He came in, didn't speak.

My mother went around busying herself more than usual and, in Johnny's presence, there was a wave of insults and ridicule. "You're going to have a baby." And mother called me all those horrible names. "And what are you going to do about it?" The horror of it made my father hysterical and my mother constantly remarked on my weight gain. I wore a large cable cardigan that Nana had knitted for me and loose, unattractive clothes.

One morning I woke up in a sweat. My body was burning up and Nana said, "Oh my God." And then after a quick inhalation of breath and a startled gasp, she put her hand on my head, "Are you all right?" I had not eaten anything since the night before. I could not look at the food without feeling sick. I had changed from childhood to womanhood and then the silences, the lies and prevarications and whispered meetings long into the night after they thought I was asleep.

Chapter 36

My hair was a tangled mop, no matter what I did, I didn't like the way I looked, the way I dressed and moved. This is what comes over us when beautiful memories shatter. I felt completely useless, unattractive, and worthless. Everyone in the house treated me like a nonentity. I was filled with resentment and became more and more inwardly restless. My whole body began to shiver. I felt afraid in anticipation of something bad that was going to happen to me. I lay there listening to the wind, feeling relieved every time it weakened and died down. My poor self-image ensnared me and crippled me.

Alongside these images I saw a pregnant adolescent who had been profoundly changed by the shattering events of the past year. About to reach motherhood, I was still a bewildered child unable to understand why my familiar world was falling apart. The baby was kicking. I felt a little arm or maybe a knee slide to the surface of my stomach. I was panting from exertion and my legs were shaking. I believed, hoped and prayed that against all the odds that all this would go away, that it was just a terrible dream. I was so desperate to cover it up.

If I exposed him I would bring the whole house down with him and how could I possibly destroy my own family in the process. This would surely kill my parents. My father was distraught, and panic was running high. Later I developed a throbbing in my stomach that came and went in uneven rhythms. Still the ache came back like something squeezing my abdomen. I got up and started to walk around to try and ease it. If this was revealed to the world outside, there would be no telling what outrage it would cause in the house so I was anxious to avoid another outburst.

The pregnancy had made me so ungainly and I was absolutely terrified of having a child and had visions of my father's anger at the taboo of an illegitimate baby. I can't remember a time in my life when I had been so lost and unkempt. I was being sick and Nana held a bowl with a gentle hand on my head and mother came in to see what all the fuss was about.

"You idiot, stupid girl," she screamed insults into my ear.

The sickness stopped. I lay back against the pillow and put my hand over the swelling. Mostly mother blamed me for being a nuisance, not being able to help out with the cleaning and the heavy jobs around the place. "I don't like your laziness," mother would say when I became lethargic and unresponsive. There was a litany of complaints about my behavior from my mother and father. They called me stupid and selfish and inconsiderate. Nothing helped gain even a shred of sympathy from either of them and I ended up hating them both. They were always moaning about something, my father's pride was wounded and I was the selfish and inconsiderate one.

No one knows what goes on behind closed doors, the violent tempers, the physical and verbal abuse I was regularly subjected to. I was constantly being asked to get up and do something. They laughed at my suffering. "You have brought it on yourself, you stupid girl,"

The whole conversation came flooding back to me. The pains came slowly at first and wouldn't rest and mother ranted around. By mid-afternoon the pains began to come faster and stronger and Nana made me as comfortable as she could but the birth was not progressing and I was exhausted. Now what I wanted was to turn back the clock never to have been born myself. Darkness came quickly and the air grew colder still. Everything that had once seemed safe and certain had unraveled before my eyes.

Chapter 37

The first rush of real pain hit me, an excruciating pain around my lower abdomen, squeezing so tightly that it felt like my insides might burst out on the floor. I felt a slow grinding ache at the bottom of my stomach, a stabbing in the lower half of my back and I let out a fast breath of pain. I could feel that the baby had moved down in my womb, its body pressing heavily on my bladder. The grinding in my stomach was back. I was doubled up. Then there was another contraction and I had to lie down. Nana helped me onto the bed and it seems to take forever. Outside it was overcast. Darkness had fallen and rain lashed at the window. It had been several hours. Lightning flashed, thunder crackled with a sound like tearing the earth apart like my body was being torn apart.

"Don't think you are entitled to a midwife. We are not calling one," my mother looked at me fiercely and kept wandering in and out of the room. Nana said she would assist at the birth. I just wanted everyone else to go away, everyone except Nana.

Then my father came into the room. "Sit up," he said. "It's Father Lynch. He has come to hear your confession." I couldn't open my mouth. What was I going to confess?

"Just repeat the words after me," Father Lynch said, pulling a purple stole around his neck and making the sign of the cross over me. I can't remember the jumble of words, something about God's forgiveness for the sins of the flesh. I wasn't listening. But I mumbled something in return and he raised his hand over me in absolution. Then he turned and went out into the kitchen without another word.

I grabbed hold of Nana's hand. and tried to count my way through it, my breath was forced out of me in a series of low moans, the pain rose, peaked, then started to ebb away.

"You can do this," Nana kept sponging my forehead.

"Shh, you can do this. Good girl, come on, take it easy," but my thoughts were blocking everything out. This time the peak lasted for ever. I tried to breathe but each gasp came out sharp and shallow, and by this time I could hear myself crying with fear, the waves of pain came in quick succession, each one fiercer that the last. Nana's voice came from somewhere a long way off. I was breathing in and out.

"That's it, good girl, and again, breathe in, out, in, out." And then suddenly it changed. Out of my exhaustion rose the most overwhelming need to push, to force it out of me. I tried to pull myself up but I couldn't make it. When the need came I pushed till there was no more breath, until my eyes watered with the strain.

"The head is there. I can see it. It's ready to come." Every limb was quivering with pain and fear. I could feel the tears running down my face. "Now push, push down for all your life. Come on yes, yes, again. It's here. It's nearly out." And I felt myself stretch to breaking point. Nana took my face in her hands and sponged the wetness away. Her hand was gentle and her voice was urgent. "One more and it will be out. Push, push, hold, push and again push."

My voice howled around the room I heard another sensation, yes out it came, a huge fast slithering power and a sense of release like nothing I had ever know before.

"Oh it's here, it has come." Out came the angry vibrating little yell, Tommy's first instant protest against the insanity and outrage of the world he had entered. Nana cut the cord. But immediately after that, he was whisked away to the other room. I was never allowed to hold him.

I was shaking so much that I could barely speak. Nana massaged my stomach to push out the afterbirth. So that was the day he was born.

Later Nana placed a small bunch of snowdrops in a jam jar of water on the window sill. The delicate smell of the flowers always reminded me of that day. Was it a boy or a girl I wondered? Then I slept the sleep of death. All the events of the previous night, from beginning to end, unfolded themselves before my tortured memory. It went from total darkness and then I noticed a feeble glow, which came through the small window. I could make out the faint light slipping into the room and the door opened suddenly.

"Where am I," I asked. "Where is the baby?"
"He didn't make it," Mother said.

"But I heard him."

"Be quiet, you heard your own screams. That's all."

But later in the day, Rosie told me how they had taken Tommy from the room minutes after he was born before I could hold him. "I heard him crying," Rosie said and I found out later that this had played on her mind for the rest of her life. "He was crying but they wrapped him up in a piece of sack and put him in the biscuit tin. Mother covered the tin in brown paper, like a parcel tied up in thick twine."

I noticed that evening that my mother's eyes were red from crying. It was getting dark and everyone was there, my parents and Johnny and Father Lynch. I was so weak and Nana helped me into the back seat with Johnny and my mother. Nana and Rosie watched from the doorway as we drove down the lane. We sat in Fr. Lynch's car, Mother with her first grandchild wrapped up in a biscuit tin, on her knee, ready to be discarded in some strange place. Johnny's baby. And my Tommy. I sat in numbed silence and no tears came.

"We will take the back road and through the side gate into the un-consecrated ground," Father Lynch spoke with authority. He was in charge of the little ritual. The snow was steadily settling but the roads still passable. Father Lynch sat with my father in front. Only the five of us at the small funeral. The snow was casting a veil over the present and the past. Within minutes we were walking through the graveyard, ankle deep in snow, wet slushy melted snow. Just coldness, a deadly coldness and emptiness in my heart.

Tommy's funeral was a secret affair, in the dead of night, in the little un-consecrated plot removed from all the other graves. They had a Christian burial ground but Tommy was in this limbo. His birth and burial had to remain hidden and sinful. The tiny parcel was lowered into the ground. Johnny carried a small wreath. It was his right. This was his baby being buried beneath the bitter snow and this is the one secret that haunts me day and night, a small group coming in with a box, in silence without a proper ceremony, lowering it into an open grave and burying it there quietly and secretly in the darkness. It was a shallow grave. It would be easy to dig it up again even with a trowel. I suppose I longed to do that but they never gave me that opportunity.

Father Lynch said some prayers asking God to drive out the devils of lust.

They lowered the box. Johnny threw the wreath down onto the biscuit tin. They couldn't allow it to be seen on top of the little mound. Someone thrust a lump of clay into my hand and I realised I was being invited to throw it into the hole. I stepped up to the edge and looked down and saw the box glowing palely in the dark. The silent scream runs on and on in my mind. I felt nauseous and the thick hedges lurched insanely. I leaned out over the edge of the pit, looked down below in the dark. I screamed in rage and fury but Johnny put his hand across my mouth.

"The villagers will hear," he snarled.

The small group was clustered around the edge of the grave and I was paralysed by the horror of it all. I tried to reach down and drag him out but a hand restrained me and I looked at the horror-struck faces around me. In the dark shadows we were walking again in a slow line towards the small gate. I shivered and the snow came down harder and I walked slowly, carrying the image of that day engraved in my mind.

This was the grief that did not age, that did not go away with time, like most grief. "Time is a great healer," people said   I found myself crying again and at the same time I thought I heard loud weeping and convulsive sobbing. I lay listening to the storm, the wind tearing at the walls of the buildings He is buried. I am buried here for the rest of my life. Never to be dug up. Terrified in the scene of my own suffering like a living death.

Tommy was still lying there in that small church yard, in that small plot of un-consecrated ground, under the pink winter jasmine tree. I remembered the exact spot. I wanted to come back but they had other plans for me. I thought I would sneak out of the house in the middle of the night and dig up his tiny box and bring him back to life with my warm milk and run away from this place forever with Tommy wrapped in a warm blanket.

The next day they came for me. They put steel handcuffs around my wrists and led me off to the van. In that cold winter day, they condemned me and cast me out.

.

Chapter 38

The day I was taken away was one of the worst days of my life and I relive this horror over and over again. I still wake up in a cold sweat every time the memories return in my nightmares. I was only sixteen. A female officer tried to handcuff me at the small half door of the farm house. She had a truncheon on her belt. She grabbed me by the arm. I kicked and flailed and bit her hand. She pulled it free and applied the handcuffs.

The worst part of that frightful day which returns so often to haunt me, is when father held me as they applied the handcuffs.

Rosie wasn't allowed to see me go but I saw Nana being pushed back through the door.
The little farm house became smaller and smaller until it vanished from sight forever.
I never saw Nana again but her voice continued to echo in my ears, vibrating in my head, the whole world shaking and on the journey everything was spreading fear as we travelled further and further into the unknown, wherever we went I had no idea at the time.

The fear of the desolation was as savage as death itself. My mind often flies back to that terrible day. It had come so suddenly and so unheralded. Just a few pieces of paper from Father Lynch and I was committed to a life of imprisonment in the asylum for the insane. There were times when the sorrows rained down on me with such force that I crumbled under their weight and couldn't make out where I was and what this was all about. Father Lynch decided what people had to believe. It was his saintly ministry. He had all the authority in my village and no one questioned his decisions.

"You will be placed in a psychiatric hospital for your own safety, and no one can say for how long. It's for your own good and what your family want for you." These were the last cruel words I heard muttered from his mouth. I started to become increasingly mistrustful and could barely speak and then I heard them murmur something about my being sectioned. I didn't know what that meant but I had heard the term used over and over again in the years that followed.

I felt something deep inside of me screaming with panic. A strange feeling of heaviness weighed down my heart and my body, draining my legs of their power. It was a feeling heavier than the weight of the whole earth. The sky also had undergone a change. Its colour turned to black, like it was pressing down upon me with its added load. I was disappearing into nothingness.

"You have nothing to fear except your own self," they told me. They said I had killed my baby and I was mad and they were going to lock me away in a madhouse. I strained to hear the things they are saying about me but can catch only a vague mumble of words.

Chapter 39

This was a bad time for me. Meg lay in the infirmary in a small cubicle, the bitter cold of the early hours getting to her living bones. She bore her pain so patiently. Dr Wynn came to have a look at her and prescribed antibiotics. She lay at her ease but in a curious say.

I sat there in the twilight of the infirmary. She had always brought the sunshine and now she brought the moonlight. Her face was so creased and old, so lost in age but she was still beautiful. The beauty of her soul still shone out of her blue eyes. We had talked so much over the years but now her voice was frail as she laid there, her long silver hair flowing freely over the pillow. She was hot, burning up and feverish. I took a damp cloth and sponged her forehead every half hour.

"I put a bunch of daffodils on Anna's grave," I said quietly, "and one on Tommy's."

"That was nice," she whispered and squeezed my hand. These were painful days. Meg was often silent, it had become too difficult to sleep. In the evening I visited her again and offered her some food which Shirley has prepared specially for her. She tried her best but could only eat very small morsels.

"You don't have to come," she told me.

"But I want to."

"Yes I know but I am no company for anyone," her voice had become a whisper.

Her face was soft, her skin transparently pale and her lovely blue eyes were beginning to lost their lustre.

I didn't know it then but this was to be the last week of her life as the pain flowed in deeper waves and drew her down. They brought in physicians to help alleviate her suffering but she had refused most of the medicines and shared her agony with no one. No one knew how long the disease had been eating into her flesh but the doctors said it was now a large tumour which was inoperable. But right from the start she was adamant that there was nothing to be done for it. In the last hours she grew crazy with pain and fever.

Meg had suffered for six weeks, a period during which I was shocked that she had lost so much weight. All the flesh in her weathered face had dropped, her lower eyelids sagged to expose a red rim, her cheeks hung loose. It was heartbreaking to watch her suffer in silence, that wonderful woman who had done nothing but help everyone, lying there in the darkness, unable to sleep, awaiting her own death.

We had made our goodbyes and sat until one of the nurses came back with a draught she had prepared. Meg took it and we sat with her until she fell into a light sleep. I sponged her brow and pushed a lock of damp hair back from her face. Her skin was glistening with sweat and tears but she still looked so peaceful. She languished for three more days, growing weaker with each one of them.

Finally she became consumed by her illness and could barely speak. She was still a handsome woman but the light in her eyes had dimmed, the sparkle had gone. I missed her quiet, shining intelligence more that I had dared let myself admit. She swallowed again, and again I lifted the glass to his mouth. She took a tiny sip, then laid her head back down and closed her eyes. I sat for a while and waiting for death to turn into life again. I saw her wince with pain. She moaned slightly, rolling sideways in her sleep.

She was so tiny. The robe they had found for her was too big for her emaciated body and her shoulders were bare. I found a light woollen blanket and placed it over her shoulders and put my arms gently around her body to give her some of my own body warmth. Her flesh was cold and still, like a corpse and she was so thin I could feel every bone through her skin. Now and then she tried to raise her head and her lungs racked with coughing. I wouldn't leave her. I just sat there reminiscing on all the good times we had together. Meg had always known what was best for me. She didn't deserve to suffer like this.

Chapter 40

Meanwhile, Angel laughed and twirled her hair around her fingers. I greeted her and an enormous pair of sad eyes stared back. It had been a losing battle getting her to eat even the tiniest morsel of food. Her face was now sunken. Her sleeves split open at the elbow like wings, the silk skirt fell like a waterfall around her legs and across the floor. She never spoke of her past. In fact in the last few years she had spoken very little at all. Once I took her small hand in mine, the nails shining and pink, transparent and cold.

I found it very difficult to understand why anyone would refuse food. Having been brought up during the war when food was so scarce, we had come to appreciate everything that was put before us. But at that time I didn't realise the seriousness of her eating disorder.

Shirley began to explain, "Anorexia is an eating disorder associated with an obsessive fear of gaining weight where you basically starve yourself." I wondered if there was anything we could do to stop this. "Angel has a strong, almost overwhelming fear of putting on weight, and is preoccupied with the size of her body. Sometimes when she is forced to eat she makes herself sick to lose weight. She has always had this constant fear of gaining weight."

I asked if she had been offered any medical help or if her condition was curable. "Matron has always tried to get the right treatment for Angel. The sooner the treatment is started, the better the chance of recovery. But sadly Angel has resisted all forms of treatment." It was clear that she was becoming very ill and she was having trouble standing unaided.

Angel was only a couple of yards away from me. Her long, shimmering silk skirts and pale skin and wraithlike body make her look like some sort of unearthly creature. The waves of chiffon seemed to capture the shine of the light. It gave her whole appearance an angelic aura. I had noticed that several of the other patients still found her strange and they would turn and gawp at her, half fascinated, half repulsed. Her underskirts were soft and full as angels' wings so that when she glided past you could hear the material sighing across the floor.

Chapter 41

There was always great excitement and curiosity in the air when a new patient arrived and this was particularly the case when Reg appeared on the scene. Two wardens chauffeured him into the exercise yard on the day after his arrival.

"He is tall, dark and handsome and gentle as a lamb," I told Shirley.

"Don't kid yourself," was all she said at the time and just walked off laughing.

Shirley always reveled in telling alarming stories, sometimes frightening us to death and even on occasions frightening herself. "Well your tall, dark and handsome stranger, gentle as a lamb is not so gentle after all. He isn't even handsome. When I saw him grin out there he showed several missing teeth and we all know how that came about! We have just got rid of Nick back to Broadmoor and now we have Reg. I have a feeling he will try to do something violent, perhaps to himself or maybe even to someone else."

"The same old story," Shirley went on. "After his treatment in Broadmoor, he is deemed to be cured and with the correct medication and constant supervision, he will not be a threat to anyone here. Who do they think they are kidding? But I guess there just aren't enough places in secure institutions for all these madmen."

Shirley was right. It was only days before we saw Reg in his true light. We heard noises outside. The men had just arrived in the exercise yard and the mood became suddenly darkened when an expression of maniacal intense hatred and fear came across Reg's wild, unnatural features, with a face full of madness and exhibitions of brutality. He burst out with a volley of abuse and curses.

"Another one for solitary confinement!" Shirley shook her head, and once she started to tell us something, there was no stopping her. She knew the whole story. He tried to murder his wife while in the grip of delusions. Then he was removed to a psychiatric unit somewhere in London.

It stems from his early childhood, when life has been unfair to him and had dealt him a severe blow. He used to hold down a well paid job. He had alcohol dependency and had been a drug user in the past. He exhibited schizophrenic tendencies but seemed to have a firm grasp of reality at most stages of his life, with the exceptions of the occasional acute panic attack."

"Reg suffers from a personality disorder and we have the extraordinary advantage of his own written account of the formative years of his life which had caused contempt for his superiors and his preferences for solitude. "But the final straw and the thing that sent him over the edge was finding out that his wife had been unfaithful to him. He discovered she was having an affair with their next door neighbour. In his murderous madness, he came out of the kitchen one evening after work with a carving knife and stabbed his wife to death. The full extent of his crimes was never proved but all the while, he showed no remorse and did not seem to understand the seriousness of his actions. You think I'm exaggerating, don't you, but it's all in the papers. I have the cuttings in that drawer at the foot of my bed.

"He was found guilty of manslaughter but not guilty of murder on the grounds of diminished responsibility. He is a potentially dangerous man who was recommended a Restriction Order under the Mental Health Act."

"But here is alongside people who have done nothing wrong, just another part of the maddening crowd."

Chapter 42

Charles looked at my notes. My case had been cut and dry, a brief account of the events that led up to my incarceration. This first copy was in a very poor state, hand-written and almost illegible. My whole life had been written on Fr. Lynch's sheets of manuscript. But Charles had made headway in collecting as much information as possible. He was determined that my case must not be treated lightly. Some further documentation had arrived and my file was beginning to fill up. There were brief notes from the days of Doctor Mac and lengthy reports written by Charles himself along with accounts given by Matron and the board of governors.

Charles was concerned about Meg and had been up to the infirmary several times to visit her. He knew that Meg's illness was heartbreaking for me, just seeing her lying there suffering and unable to do anything to alleviate her pain. She was gasping for breath while her life slid silently away as I fed her morphine from a spoon. I remember the gentle lament of her pain. One morning as I sat holding her hand, she was grabbed by a convulsion, then a fit of wheezing and coughing. I bathed her hot skin through the night and gave her water on a sponge. With eyes shrunken and shriveled into their sockets, her face gazed towards the spring blossoms outside the window on the tall trees.

The moon shone on Meg's face. Like a vision from heaven she lay there on her small iron bed in the infirmary, skin glowing pale in the weak light. Her health was deteriorating by the hour. She lay lifelessly still. Without warning I burst into tears. The tears ran down my face and I tried to hide them behind my hands. Despite her weakness, Meg took hold of both my hands and lifted them softly away from my face. "I need to cry," I told her. A lot of old memories came tumbling into my mind, mainly Rosie and Nana. I wish I could have been with Nana for her passing. No doubt she had gone to her reward a long time ago.

I remembered a particular day when Meg twisted her hands together on the table and looked at me. "Are you all right to go on?" she asked. I nodded. I could not stop talking because now I had started to tell her my story, I wanted it to be finished. "I don't know how these people got away with it," she handed me a tissue and wiped her own eyes. She sat down next to me and she put her hand on my shoulder.

"To survive you must look good and speak well," she used to tell me and that was before she had me reading and discussing all sorts of topics. Prior to that I did not smile or even look in any man's face. I was terrified until late at night after they locked the men away and I was able to relax.

"Something fine will happen to you," Meg used to say. "Something marvellous, and you will forget some of the bad times. Her story was as sad as mine but she learned to overcome much of her unhappiness. She shook his head. "Life can be like a bad dream or something that we should just try and shake away."

Like Meg, I learned to live a fairly peaceful and placid life and now when I looked back on all those years, I knew that in inexpressible ways she was very, very dear to me. We had developed kindred minds and spirits. I came to life at her touch. When we were together, we were always happy, always smiling, not like everyone else around us, as if a cloud had lifted and there was something else, some sort of revelation, like a glimpse of God, some reassurance, a hint of something beyond our understanding, bigger than both of us.

But Meg was no longer able to walk or talk. She cried softly when she was in pain and slept when she was not. When she breathed there was a rasping, echoing sound that reverberated round her chest. She had no solid food for weeks, couldn't swallow any more, and the best we could do was to get a little water into her mouth.

"The illness has gone to her chest," the doctors said, "and the danger is that pneumonia will set in." She was emaciated and we all knew she was nearing her end. Her breathing became laboured and we watched the last remnants of her strong body slowly wither. It was painful to see her suffer, her face contorted in pain

We feared greatly that Meg might die in the night but day broke cold and cheerless with the same clouded sky and beating wind and roaring seas. She had made it to another day. We wanted to be with her to hold her hand so that she would not die alone. It was early evening, the rays of the setting sun over the church tower were now shining on Meg's pillow. What a night! I'll never forget it no matter how long I live, memories dominated by sleeplessness and pain all around. Meg was breathing her last. Everything was enormous, the gown she wore, the wedding ring slack on her finger. I was with her to the end along with Shirley and Matron. None of us would leave her bedside. When the final hour came, a doctor took the stethoscope and sounded her heart. He held my hand gently, and then turned to Shirley and Matron. "Her suffering is over." He gently closed her eyes, those blue eyes that would never smile at me again.

Meg's body was washed and she was dressed in her favourite blue smock covered in little white flowers. She was gently laid out in the chapel where her body remained for a day while some of the other patients came to pay their respects. Before the lid was finally fitted on the coffin, I bent down and kissed the top of her head. Meg's death blew a cold wind through all our lives.

I imagined the chapel was filled with a heavenly scent, of lilac and lavender, geraniums and sunflowers and in my memory the seasons had all run into each other.

She was buried in the atmosphere she would have wished, refusing to be parted from her friends. It was her wish to rest there amongst them. A proper tombstone was erected as she slept the eternal sleep amongst all those nameless tombstones. Though it was early spring, there was an almond tree flowering already, to guide us to her eternal resting place.

Kathy Lavelle

Chapter 43

It was Christmas day and the first fall of snow. The morning passed so peacefully but the day ended in sadness. Christmas lights were on all through the building, the whole place illuminated and there was a radiance of stars and everything was bright against the coming dark of winter. The traditional Nativity scene had been erected, surrounded by wreaths of holly and mistletoe. This was always Angel's favourite part of the Christmas season. She used to spend hours gazing at the figures in the manger but her favourite was the Angel Gabriel on top of the crib.

The dining room looked beautiful with an enormous Christmas tree in the large bay window. Everyone loved the traditional ways, the church, the goose, the chocolate. December was always a time of darkness and now we had this wonderful festival of light. It looked warm everywhere, almost intimate with candles burning in the kitchen on the advent window, giving off a rose glow. Everything smelled of Christmas, from the pine tree to the mulled wine that was being served. Everyone seemed to be on their best behaviour, laughing, smiling, teasing, and giving out little presents, making everything a little brighter.

This was likely to be my last Christmas in "The Manor," full of good things and also full of promise of new beginnings. Charles told me I would be going home in the springtime but this filled me with a sort of sadness, going out into the unknown. I wondered what it would be like next year. The air was still cold, but it was clear and frosty and the sky was a bright piercing blue. I tried to push away the ache in my heart when I thought of all my sleepless nights and my new fears of the unknown.

That evening Angel had been moved down to the medical ward. She was so fragile now and her life was balanced between life and death. She was under close supervision but still refused food and drink. She pulled the intravenous drips from her arm and oxygen mask from her face. Her breathing was strained but she still would not accept help.

In the afternoon I went to visit Meg's grave. It was the shadowy darkness of a December afternoon. In this deepest gloom, it would be easy to slip in these gates in the twilight. Some old twist of bushes and paths and lonely things were all now buried in the snow. I took calm from the spreading path the quiet stones and the familiar number of iron tags. There were the pillars and the old sharp arch with its faded figures. The world was clean with the whiteness of the snow wiping away all sadness.

I took the angel down from the crib and went to visit Angel on Christmas evening. She smiled and stroked the angel and I left it there on her pillow. She lay still in her flowing silks and looked so angelic, like the angel she always claimed to be.

I wept, not so much for Angel as I knew she was going to a better place, but for myself and my feelings of guilt because I had been unable to help her.

Chapter 44

The music in the kitchen on Boxing Day was beautiful and peaceful, everything quiet out of respect for Meg. But a strange thing had happened. Angel had gained some unexplained new strength and had escaped out of her sick bed unnoticed and out into the snow. We all went about our daily tasks totally oblivious of her absence. They say that a strange strength returns just immediately before death. That is the only explanation we could give later.

Shirley wanted to tell me all about the illness. "We have another sick person in our midst. You know Angel is seriously ill. She has been ill for a long time and everyone has tried to help her eat something,"

"It's not as easy as that. Treatment is very complex and varies depending on the individual circumstances. Some people have been treated for anorexia but there is no one single treatment that has proven to be effective in all cases and impossible to find the right treatment for our little Angel. The doctors and staff have aimed to restore her to a healthy weight, by helping her to develop healthy eating patterns. But nothing has worked. As well as the physical complications Angel has associated mental health problems with her own thoughts, feelings and beliefs concerning food and body image. In addition to treatment by the medical doctors, when possible she has had help from a psychiatrist who has experience in eating disorders."

"But none of this has helped Angel. It's not that she isn't hungry. She is starving. She would rather die than eat a cheese sandwich. She feels that if she eats she will put on weight. If she puts on weight she will go totally out of control. She will grow and grow and grow. And everything that she is terrified of will happen. Angel doesn't have a problem with being fat. She has a problem with being woman-sized. Becoming a woman means growing up, trying to have relationships. She had always been indifferent to the praise or criticism of colleagues, teachers or friends at every stage in her life. She had very low self-esteem and this is the thing that went wrong for her when she was a young girl and what brought about that brutal murder of her pimp. Her condition is frightening for all of us. For Angel it is petrifying. Starving makes time stand still. She used to eat a bowl of cereal a day. Now she eats nothing. When she starves herself she is somebody but it fills all of us around her with fear and frustration."

"Generally, people can't understand why she won't eat. They say, 'It's easy, all you have to do is pick up a knife and fork'. They don't understand and it is hard to explain the fear she has. How can she tell them she would rather die than be a normal adult weight and shape? When she looks in the mirror Angel sees a fatty. She is blind to the hip bones and the ribs sticking out all over the place. She hides under huge jumpers or massive coats so that people don't notice. She tells herself, "When I don't eat I am in control, when I am thin I am safe." So in spite of this extreme weight loss, Angel believes she is fat and is terrified of becoming what is in fact a normal weight or shape. About four out of ten people with fully established anorexia make a complete recovery, and others improve but we have seen no improvement with Angel and now everyone knows that she will not recover."

"We all know that Angel's eating disorders have developed as a result of difficult life experiences. She was under social pressures when growing up but then disaster struck. She had been physically and sexually abused and this caused her to commit those terrible crimes. Angel is depressed and has her own obsessions. Everyone has tried to help. Although we can begin to understand why the illness developed it seems impossible to help her to overcome it. The long-term aims of the doctors and staff were to help Angel change her attitudes and behaviour, to change her ways of thinking, and enable her to cope with the strains of life without the illness as a protection."

I did not know that Angel had tried to commit suicide twice and everyone feared that she would succeed eventually. Her grandmother had taken her own life and they say that there is a suicide gene, passed down the generations. I wished we could do something to help Angel.

I was still missing Meg dreadfully and wandered through the gates into the church and cleared the snow off the small bench beside Meg's grave. The graveyard was always awash with colourful plants, season by season. In springtime, there were lilac bushes and a flowering cherry tree, a hawthorn hedge and a high wall dividing it from the wheat field which rolled on into other wheat fields, potato fields, oilseed rape fields on and on to the horizon. In summer it grew roses in abundance, lavender, columbines, poppies, pansies, clematis, snapdragons, wallflowers and forget-me-nots. And winter brought the most beautiful pink and yellow jasmine shrubs in sheltered corners decorating many of the graves. I often went there to meditate. All those people lying there have their own story, each unique. And they were all being celebrated and blessed by the amazing prolific gifts of nature.

Meg had been gone for nearly a year. I brushed the snow off the bench, sat down under the winter jasmine. Wrapped in a thick cloak with woollen hat and scarf, I sat there and sorted through my memories but the harder I tried to remember the more I got confused about which are memories and which are stories.

Everything was deep in snow. I whispered a silent prayer for Meg and all these others with their own stories and this breathed a spirit of new hope into my senses, a hope which these people never enjoyed. As I sat there, I knew Charles was working tirelessly for my release. The clouds overshadowing me will be dispersed. My heart was filled with optimism and I knew Meg was looking out for me still.

In the glimmering light, I fancied I saw something strange, tumbling quickly down across a tombstone, floating and insubstantial, a living creature, out there in the snow. I jumped up. "Angel," I cried.

She looked at me with eyes like stars. She was playing hide and seek in her bare feet in the snow with little singing and clapping games and running here and there like a small child. In a way she was so beautiful and so innocent, so angelic.

But I felt a tremor in my hands as I looked at her again. It was cold and an icy wind came up from the sea but Angel was oblivious of all that, dressed in her beautiful long chiffon dress and sleeves flapping like wings. I imagined I saw her fly across to a statue of the Angel Gabriel at the upper end of the cemetery.

She gave a sort of dance around the statue and then gently spread her body over the angel wings and just lay there. I walked toward her but all was still. She lay there so peacefully, an angel in all her glory. Just then a procession of nurses in white uniforms and the Vicar in his long white robes came through the small gate. They had been searching everywhere for her and then found her tiny footprints in the snow. They had come for Angel but she had gone to her home with the Angel Gabriel, like she always said she would.

Kathy Lavelle

Chapter 45

Charles came back the following week.   We talked about the absolute power and corruption of such people as Father Lynch. For me now he is a savage man from the darkest corner of the earth, the greatest demon, a man of God, who was supposed to protect me and give me spiritual guidance, was himself a man of evil whose only wish was to satisfy his own selfish needs. He was the voice of the judge and jury, announcing my execution.   No words could describe my feelings for this man.

A deep feeling of something frightening came into my mind. I was screaming, screaming, for mercy, from God, for Tommy. A cold creeping feeling came into my brain and a physical pain. The pain of childbirth is said to be one of the worst pains anyone can endure. They say the pain is soon forgotten once the baby is born. But I wasn't allowed to keep the baby. The pain of childbirth has stayed with me all these years.   Maybe the only good thing Father Lynch did was to commit me to the asylum. I can't begin to think what would have happened if I had stayed back there in the midst of those evil people. I started to cry inwardly, not for myself strangely enough, but for Rosie and Nana who had to live on with them

I used to fancy I actually saw people who weren't there, little tricks of my imagination. But in my mind I was suddenly back with Michael, the trouble being, it was getting harder to picture him. It was so long ago and he didn't seem real any more.   I was searching for the stream that ran through the middle of the woods where we could guess the time of day from the height of the sun and then make our way home, late and footsore, to the mooing of the cows waiting to be milked.

"You have been lost in your thoughts," I was suddenly aware that I was in the room with Charles.

I'll never see Nana again at home or anywhere else on the face of the earth. How can I have a home without her? What has become of all the hopes attached to her and all because I had just disappeared from her life, with no one until now to speak up for justice, locked away for a lifetime, a life sentence, silenced forever by Father Lynch.

"Only God knows the whole story," Charles was breaking into my thoughts again, "and can easily catch people out in their falsehood. It has all been so dark, so difficult for you but there is light at the end of the tunnel,"

The night was tranquil. It was dark everywhere, rays of light were flashing in the darkness and I was happy again about everything, It was like a new dawn when darkness was slowly giving birth to light, and the waiting I had endured all night was now over. I knew Tommy was at rest and no one could ever hurt him again. I had attained a certain degree of composure and tranquillity. Charles had lifted the veil from my eyes, like a light suddenly glowing in the darkness. Rays from the sun streamed back into my life.

Chapter 46

It was not so much a question of whether people doubted that what I had written was the truth about myself but the certainty in my own mind that what I wrote and said was absolutely true down to the finest detail, the incident in the kitchen over the biscuit tin, my friendship with Meg, my longing for Nana. My memories had carried me back and forth in time and it seems I was fated to record the dismaying horrors of the hillside.

I might have killed him with whatever implement I could find. I might have torn a stone from a wall, a stick from a fence and battered him to death, the death he deserved. I saw myself as a little girl sitting with my doll in the window, the doll he had bought for me, trapped indoors by the storm. Sometimes a new wave of strength came over me and I knew I would have the strength to kill him. I knew I could snatch at something, a rock or sharp piece of slate and gladly murder him. I don't know why I did not. My punishment would not have been any greater, as it was, the whole village was murmuring against me, the mad woman. What difference would it have made if they had gone around with the outcry, murderer?

"What's the date," Charles asked with a sort of vagueness on his face.

"Seventh of January," I said. I'm never sure of the date but I always knew this one.

Reading my mind Charles said, "You always know this date?" Then I stopped. I had said too much already.

"Is it a significant date?" he probed. I was silent. The fact is we are missing so many threads in our stories that the tapestries are bound to fall apart. He looked at me, waiting for an answer. Finally I told him that the sixth of January was the day of Tommy's birth. The feast of the Epiphany and the three wise men. I thought of the irony, the three wise men, my father, Johnny and Father Lynch. Three wise men had brought gifts to the Infant Jesus, gold, frankincense and myrrh. But these men murdered my baby and put him in a dark place.

" I don't intend to throw you out into the cold, hostile world," Charles went on but a feeling of seeping dread spread through my body, like a sickness or memory of a sickness, the first time in many years I had felt it.

"Of course I want freedom but it frightens me."

"The gaining of freedom is always accomplished in an atmosphere of uncertainty," he said and went on trying to reassure me.

He stopped speaking then and I gazed at the solid rectangle of sunlight in the room. "I know nothing of this life outside or my family." I tried to speak calmly although at this moment I was feeling anything but calm

"I have unexpectedly found some additional material," he said. "I don't know whether it will help us as it pertains to matters in the long ago, but certain information has come to light, notes that had been transferred here with you. Under the new law, we have to assess which patients can be put back into the community, but in your case there is no question of your release." I was concerned that they would find me an unworthy candidate to release back into the world. Perhaps they thought some of my actions were the work of a lunatic, maybe they thought I was still mad after the incidents where I was lying in the snow on the sixth of January and still screaming in the night and crazy on Christmas day when the only thing to set me crazy was the cook opening a tin of biscuits.

Dr. Mac doubted my story. "Something doesn't ring true," he said. "Memory is a very unreliable thing. Many memories of traumatic events can be unreliable, or just a figment of one's imagination. We must take everything we think we remember with a pinch of salt?" Then he talked about the issue of false memories.

"I have been writing a thesis on memory," he said. "We now know a great deal about memory and are learning more every day. Memory is a tricky thing, often untrustworthy and even changeable. There is no doubt, however, that the process of repression, the forgetting of traumatic events, is a real and provable process." He was merely reading some gibberish from his thesis or from a psychology book.

"The process of psychotherapy is fraught with historical inaccuracies," there he was again looking down and reading from the papers on his desk. "These small distortions of the truth," he said, "have little effect on the healing power of psychotherapy, but no one should take what is remembered or talked about in the context of psychotherapy as historical truth. How we experienced the past is far more important to the process of psychotherapy than verifying each and every detail. Life consists of shades of grey. Almost nothing is absolute, at least here on this planet." He went on and on.

"But your case is different.   You are not trying to suppress memories but it is possible that your memories are constructions made in accordance with your present needs, desires and influences, Memories are often accompanied by feelings and emotions. On the other hand, if the brain is healthy and a person is fully conscious when experiencing some trauma, the likelihood that they will forget the event is practically zero, unless either they are very young or they experience a brain injury."

I think someone had told him about my nightmares and my screaming in the night. He had his dissertation in front of him, ran his finger down the side of the page and continued reading. I just sat there numbed until he slammed his notes closed.

"You can go now,"   he said and he looked up from his reading. But that was a long time ago. I remember how Shirley led me shivering into the warmth of the kitchen and poured hot chocolate into my mug. She had heard it all before and had nothing good to say about Doctor Mac. But I had real memories of a past when we were young and had Rosie and Nana who loved me, each in her own very different way.

"You were concerned that you heard your baby cry after he was born. I am trying to establish the truth of the matter," Charles said. He read the notes from Matron about the incident in the kitchen and my frightening experience in the snow on Tommy's little garden but only shook his head. He took the newspaper article out of my files. "A serial sexual predator who stalked and attached women over a twelve year period was jailed for life yesterday and was told by a judge his actions were utterly degrading, humiliating and terrifying and left his victims living in fear. They sentenced the forty-four year old priest who was convicted of twenty eight sex attacks over a number of years." This was Johnny's friend Father Lynch.

"This priest led a double life," Charles read from the cutting. "He seemingly led a normal life ministering to his parishioners. He was charming and pleasant to everyone. He expressed deep regret for his actions, but wasn't it his job to protect the vulnerable?"

"You won't see me for a couple of weeks," Charles said, "until I am able to bring things to a resolution and then make arrangements for the future. I intend to visit your sister so the next time I see you I should have a lot more information for you after I attempt to fit together some of the missing pieces of the jigsaw.

Exactly two weeks later I saw Charles again and his face was lit up with excitement.

"Good news," he said. "I found your sister Rosie alive and well. She is married to Paul and they have two delightful children, Molly who is seven years old and Daniel who is five."

I just sat there gasping at the news and shaking uncontrollably. Charles held my hand. He was not behind his desk any more but sat in a chair facing me. "Take it easy," he said and he just sat there waiting and giving me time to regain some of my composure. Finally he told me they were living back in the home place which they had totally rebuilt. "And there will be space for you. They are considering adding an extension which will be part of the main building but completely self contained with its own entrance. I think you will be surprised when you see the place."

"But that's not all," he said. "I also visited Brian, the new parish priest. It was important to find out how much he knew and get his perceptions of what had transpired all those years ago. Brian is the most charming man and was aware of the whole story. He told me he was totally appalled and embarrassed by the reports on the crimes of Father Lynch, a fellow priest. He apologised on behalf of the church."

"Rosie is a witness to what happened on that shocking night. She has testified that the baby was not stillborn. Father Lynch had covered himself. No one could point a finger or prove it one way or another or so he thought. Rosie told me that your Nana had claimed over the years that a total injustice had been done. No one could prove anything now, Father Lynch thought. There weren't any witnesses. But there were. Rosie is a reliable witness and Nana had given her a written statement for her safekeeping.

"Rosie is going to write to you, very soon." Justice has been done. God is good. Persistence has always been one of Charles's most admirable characteristics. He wouldn't give in until he had gathered the last shred of information and had left no stone unturned to search for truth and justice.

Rosie's letter arrived a week later. This was the first letter I had ever received.

Shirley handed it to me one morning when I came into the kitchen. I just stared at the postmark and stroked the blue envelope. I slipped it into my pocket and held it close to my body. It was like some ghost out of the past. After lunch Shirley looked at me as I held it close.

"Go into your room and read it. Go on girl. You need time alone."

I opened it with trembling hands.

Dearest Kathy,

I don't know if ever you will find it in your heart to forgive me. I am sorry I have not been a good sister to you but I will try to explain and I will make it up to you from now on.

So many things have happened since that terrible day when they sent you away. I wasn't even allowed to say goodbye. They banished me to the bedroom and when I came out you had gone. There was such a silence in the house. They packed me off to bed without a word of comfort. You have no idea how much I missed you. It was so cold. I wanted to put my arms around you but you weren't there. That night our little bed seemed too big without you. Nana took me into her bed and I wept silently into the pillow. I know Nana was crying too. I could hear her quiet sobs. She was heartbroken and your leaving totally destroyed her.

Your presence had been the backdrop of my life since I was a baby and you could not begin to imagine what the silence was like. The house began to echo around me and there was only Nana who understood how I felt. I don't know if you will ever be able to forgive me for not getting in touch. The truth is they said letters were banned and anyway it would only upset you if we were allowed to write. Then everything started to change for me too. My life became one of total misery. Nana told me about the things that Johnny had done to you but I was too young to fully understand.

Fr. Lynch came and arranged for me to be sent to the orphanage. It wasn't a real orphanage. It was a boarding school but they agreed to take a few girls at the request of the clergy. The majority of the girls were weekly boarders and the rich girls got all the privileges but after a while I made friends with Moira and she took me home for weekends. It was only then that life took on some semblance of normality. But I had no real freedom until I was sixteen and able to fend for myself. I worked hard and was determined that they would not destroy my soul. I passed some exams in typing and shorthand, got a secretarial post and went home only for funerals.

Dear Nana passed away peacefully in her sleep in January 1959. I think Mother showed her a lot of kindness in the final years of her life. It was at Nana's funeral that Dad told me you were dead. I will spare you the details of how I felt that day and how I reacted afterwards.

Then I met and married Paul in 1960. Our children Molly and Daniel are now aged seven and five respectively and we are very much looking forward to seeing you. They are longing to have a real auntie for the first time. Michael was already married in 1959 to our cousin Joanna Daly. He was totally distraught after you left. No one had given him any explanation of what had happened. All he knew was that you had been sent to a mental asylum in Yorkshire but he knew full well that you were not insane in any way. Three years ago Joanna was diagnosed with lung cancer and gave up her fight for life after a very short illness. Uncle Johnny died the year after you left.

Charles will give you my version of the memories of that dreadful night which haunted me continuously after you were taken away. I went to visit Nana when I had left school. She said if ever I saw you again, to tell you that she prayed for justice every day and that one day in some other happier place we would all meet up again, you and me and Tommy and her. She said we must never let your memory fade.

I am sorry to bring you all this sad news but I asked Charles to break it to you gently before you received my letter. You will already know that Mother and Dad died three years ago within nine days of each other. It was such a traumatic time but Michael and his family were so supportive. After our parents' death Paul rebuilt the old farm house and we moved back home.

I will tell you everything when we meet up again. This place is our joint inheritance. We are building an extension for you so that you can have your own independence for as long as you want and later on you can decide on where you want to live.

Father Brian, our new Parish Priest has been very supportive and knows everything. I often go up to the cemetery and put flowers on Tommy's grave when no one is watching.

I had no idea you were still alive and look forward to seeing you again soon.

Yours,

Rosie

Kathy Lavelle

Chapter 47

Shirley read the letter too with tears in her eyes and the next day Charles and I talked in great length about everything that had happened. "Johnny's ghost has finally been laid to rest. He will never hurt anyone again," I said and I pressed Nana's ring on my finger.

"Sit down," Charles said. This may come as a shock to you. "There is more press coverage about Fr. Lynch but I can't hide this information from you." I looked at the paper spread across his desk and Charles turned my attention to the startling news about Fr. Lynch. It was all there again in black and white, huge headlines once more blazoned across the newspaper. 'PRIEST PAEDOPHILE'. There was another picture of Fr. Lynch in his clerical robes. The press wouldn't let it go.

"Justice has finally been done," Charles said as we stared in disbelief at the article. "I feel humiliated and devastated about what happened, but I'm just so relieved you are getting another chance with your life," Charles looked up with pain in his eyes.

The article gave more shocking details of the extent of the crimes. "In court Fr. Lynch had pleaded guilty of raping an eight-year-old girl and was jailed indefinitely despite the fact this victim has not been identified. It is hard to believe that a man of the cloth could commit such repugnant crimes."

The court also heard that Lynch had taken a series of photos in the boys' changing rooms where he had helped coach the football team. Hundreds of indecent photos of children were found in a collection of boxes in his dark room. He was described in court as a predatory paedophile and sexual pervert who had targeted young people and vulnerable single parents to get close to their children. "He was devious and manipulative. His motives were sinister. Under the guise of being a friendly and charming man with a sympathetic ear he turned his attention to their children," Charles read in shocked horror.

"Parents had even trusted him to baby sit. He groomed one girl by giving her sweets and toys. Lynch has harboured a deep-seated sexual craving for children. It may only be as these children mature and get older that they will suffer the real scars of the abuse."

"Lynch will now remain in prison indefinitely but the judge stressed there was no guarantee he would ever be considered safe for parole. He was ordered to sign the Sex Offenders Register for life. Lynch had been described as a pillar of the community in a position of trust. Let's just say that in Lynch's case there have been in excess of twenty victims, boys and girls and that the alleged abuse dates back to the 1950s."

Charles looked in shocked horror at the evidence. "Child abuse for anyone is a despicable act, but by an ordained priest, a man of God, what can I say? And you Kathy have been blameless, wrongly committed but you are nearer to becoming a free woman at last. I apologise. I apologise on behalf of my profession."

"Everyone has failed you Kathy, home, school, society, the church and we have failed you too. For fifteen years you have been locked away for a crime you didn't commit." Charles seemed to be apologising for the faults of the whole world.

I sat there thinking. I was part of the emotional landscape of long ago, now eradicated by death and ruin. I would have to reconstruct my life. My opinion of the human race had changed radically. I was not the only person who had been wrongly accused and punished for crimes they had not committed. I dreamed of it sometimes, the old world always the same dream, the day of my departure, it might seem as though it was getting back to normal, but that was an illusion. I remember this as a confused, bewildering time, a time of new beginnings, when my fractured life had somehow to be patched up, leaving imprisonment and friends behind while a life of liberty lay before me.

Charles was writing notes in my file. He looked up at me again. "In another few months you will leave this place forever," he put down his pen and smiled across at me. This brought a sweet nostalgia to my eyes and I was fifteen again, set free and carried from strength to strength

Charles was speaking again, "When you protest against your unjust incarceration, you will have a right to demand compensation for the wasted years of your life."

"But I can't honestly say that these years have been wasted. For many patients this may be true but not for me."

"But you must have a passionate and justified sense of the wrongs you have suffered. There was no way out of the trap once the doctors in those early days had called you mad."

"In some ways it is as if I had moved here of my own accord and voluntarily subjected myself to the system as a sort of mediation. I know you say I have spent my life paying for a crime I didn't commit but this had become a safe place in which I have sought refuge and into which I could escape with my whole being."

Charles shook his head. "You are now to be a free woman and we must prepare you for life back in the real world and despite what you say, you will be compensated. I will see to that." I thanked Charles and left him still writing in my files and rushed to the kitchen to see if Shirley had read the latest news about Fr. Lynch. I opened the door but stopped in my tracks. Shirley was placing the large tin of biscuits on the worktop. I felt my whole body going into spasms of hysteria.

Shirley saw me looking at the biscuit tin. "Kathy. What is it? I thought you had got over this, put the whole thing to rest especially after Rosie's letter." She held me tightly in her arms. All the anger and grief which had been bottled up, came flooding out.

I wrenched myself from Shirley's arms and swiped the biscuit bin from the shelf spilling its contents across the floor and rushed out the door screaming down the path towards Tommy's little memorial garden. It was only a small garden but it was the centre of my universe. It was raining. I started digging up the soil with my bare hands. My whole body was covered in the wet mud. Exhausted I just lay there in a heap. The whole thing was so bizarre and it had all happened so quickly. I seem to have lost all control of my senses. My hands, face and clothes were sodden with the wet mud and I must have passed out.

When I came to, I was back in my room. "What you need is a nice hot bath," Matron said.

"And a nice hot drink," Shirley added.

I looked up at Shirley and didn't know how anyone could ever excuse such mad outbursts.
Yes now they all know. I am truly the mad person everyone said I was.

"Come on, let's help you get back to your old self," Shirley raised me gently by the hand.

Chapter 48

Charles will have heard of my mental outburst. "That's it! I won't be going anywhere. I've proved without doubt that I am mad, just like they all said I was and this is where I will stay, locked up in a mad house for the rest of my days.

Charles had sent for me. "You have bottled up too much for too long. And this is part of the grieving stages. You have lost Tommy, your parents, your Nana and recently Meg. This is too much grief for one person to bear all at once. There are five stages of grief," he added. "Having a good understanding of those five stages can help you to better understand the emotions that you are going through."

"The first stage is denial and that is what you have been feeling since you heard from Rosie. It's the stage of not being able to really admit to yourself what is going on...

The second stage is anger and this is a stage that we all have to go through if we're going to process our grief over the loss. Unfortunately, a lot of people are afraid of anger both their own anger and the anger of others, so they refuse to acknowledge this part of the process. Failure to allow yourself to feel your anger can result in never actually completing the grief process and therefore being unable to move on. It's important that you acknowledge and accept your anger over the situation. It is nothing to be ashamed of.

The third stage of grief that we go through when we experience any loss is bargaining. In the case of a death, we try to bargain with God or whatever greater spirit we believe in to try to make the big problem go away. This is typically considered to be the third stage of grief but it may come before the anger for a lot of people as they try to move out of their denial.

After all of the denial and the anger and the bargaining have been done and we realize that things really are starting to end, we become depressed. We feel helpless and powerless and overwhelmed with sadness about the loss that we are experiencing. This is the fourth stage. We feel like things will never be the same. This is the time that it is most important to make sure that we are taking care of ourselves. And we need to force ourselves to go out and do things that interest us even though this feels like the last thing that we want to do. Even as we do all this, we need to acknowledge our depression. We need to admit to our emotions. We need to cry. To deal with loss, we have to feel the terrible pangs of sadness that come along with that loss. Depression is a powerful emotion, but it'll eventually pass.

And the fifth stage is acceptance. At the end of all of this, you will eventually reach a day when you have accepted the situation. No matter how many times you pass back and forth between the different stages, you will one day find that those stages are finally done."

I looked at Charles in wonder and admiration.

"I was so ashamed of my outburst yesterday, and now I am being told it is all quite normal."

"Absolutely!"

"And now let me get off my soap box. Let's move on. Nothing has changed since we last met. Justice is on your side and your release is imminent. What seems unusual in your case is the length of time you have been trapped in the claws of an inflexible asylum system and this shows how easy it was in the past for a sane person to be admitted as insane into a psychiatric institution.

Chapter 49

It was springtime and the day of my departure and I had been up since five, filled with emotion, excitement mixed with fear and trepidation. I tried to linger over the ritual of hygiene. My head was in a whirl. I took a long shower in the bathroom down the hall. Then I was dressed and sitting in my own favourite chair in the kitchen.

Shirley wanted me to have a full English breakfast but I had no appetite. "Sorry Shirley. I couldn't eat a thing. A quick coffee and I'll be on my way." I told her. This parting was not easy. We had to wrench ourselves from the long embrace. Shirley was wiping her eyes with the tail of her apron. I turned around. It was best to go quickly.

Poor old Shirley. Over the past weeks she had tried so hard to get me to change my mind. She was such a dear friend and to be honest, I was torn between staying where I was now happy and secure and going out there into some strange new world.

One morning she said, "Sometimes I wonder if there are as many mad people out there as there are in here. We haven't been too bad. Have we?" She was joking in a way but I knew there was some element of truth in that remark. I no longer knew the difference between madness and sanity.

"It won't be easy you know," she told me only a few days before I left, "adjusting, and getting back into the swing of things. They say it is rare for a patient to readjust successfully to normal life after a period spent in a mental institution. You cannot imagine how lonely and helpless you could be on the outside after fifteen years in a place like this. Can you imagine going into the city for the first time, to go shopping. Everyone staring."

"But things have changed for everyone else too," I said.

"Yes but for them, things have evolved slowly, bit by bit over the years. You will witness change in one fell sweep. Fifteen years change in one day. Just think of the shock it could be. A job will be difficult at your age. You cannot imagine how lonely and helpless one can be on the outside after fifteen years in this place."

I know she was heartbroken. She had lost Meg and now I was going. And there was a strange tugging at my own heartstrings. Maybe she was right. After so many years in this strange place, I knew the changes in the outside world only from books and newspapers. But I had confidence in knowing that there would always be a welcome for me if I decided to come back.

"I'll be off," I said but I couldn't look back. Matron stood at the front door. I did my best to pretend that I was fine.

"Keep in touch," Matron said. We had done all our talking over the previous weeks.

"Yes I certainly will. And thanks for everything."

Charles had offered to drive me home. He felt it was his duty since he had been instrumental in arranging my release. Although I didn't want to accept his generous offer, I knew it would be good to travel with someone who knew my whole story and who could help me bridge the gap across this wide chasm.

Before I had time to show any more emotion, he beckoned me towards the car. It was a fine, long black car. I couldn't even hear the engine as we drove slowly through the gates. I waved back to the small group in the doorway. I looked back for one last time. This was the journey from one world to another.

"Are you all right?" Charles asked, placing his hand gently on my shoulder. I just nodded and stared at the narrow roads ahead. It was strange how my feelings for Charles had changed from a childish infatuation into a deep friendship. Meg was right when she said my feelings would change if I only had a little patience and didn't make a fool of myself.

Then we were off, Charles concentrating on the narrow twists and turns of the mountainous roads. Sometimes dense forests grew up from the slopes. Then the narrow roads were bordered with tall lime trees, spring foliage glistening in the early morning sun. Everything was fresh and green against distant mountains. There was an extra greenness in the grass, a softness in the light.

New life everywhere. I was bubbling over with exhilaration and trepidation. It had been a long time. I was deep in thought. Then Charles was speaking again. "Meg told me you have started to write your story."

"Yes but that was only to occupy my time. And to be honest I did it to please Meg. She had been so kind to me. She had done such a lot to turn my life around."

"But your story is worth telling," he said.

"Who would want to read it? What I have already started is not worth the paper it is written on?"

"But yours is a story of historical events in a changing world. It is about the miscarriage of justice. Many people are interested in that sort of thing. Yours is an inspirational story of strength and courage. A story of survival."

"Meg always said a good story needs a beginning, a middle and an end. My story hasn't got an end."

"But it will have a happy ending. I'm convinced of that."

I wasn't so sure. We left it at that and I quickly changed the subject. I asked Charles about the journey and how long it would take. Then we talked about his family, about his story. A new world was opening up in front of my eyes, a world which for me had not existed before and as the roads got wider, the deep blue of the sky rose up suddenly in front of us. Charles pointed out the signs for the motorway. I had seen motorways on TV but I had never been on one.

As we drove down the slip road and entered the motorway, a great surge of traffic engulfed us. All I heard was a roar of motors. The roads squirmed with traffic and Charles' attention was devoted to avoiding hitting anyone or being hit. There was so much agitation, horns blaring and lights changing, and indicators switching on and off in quick succession. I had seen horrendous traffic accidents on TV, small cars crushed underneath huge trucks, rows of ambulances and police cars. With all this in mind, I clung desperately to my seat.

At first the traffic struck me like a tidal wave of cars, trucks, station wagons and an enormous cement mixer on wheels, its big drums revolving as it drove along. Trucks as long as freighters went roaring by followed by huge overland caravans. There were huge, scary monsters of trucks with air brakes and power-assisted steering, sometimes as much as forty feet long. Civilization had certainly made great strides in my absence.

Charles' eyes were darting from road to rear-view mirror in an effort to keep clear of the enormous volume of traffic. We whizzed along in silence for most of the time.

"These great roads are wonderful for moving goods but not for enjoying the views of the countryside," I finally ventured to speak.

"You'll be ok. I promise," Charles said. "And I know what we can do. For the second part of the journey, I will stay as much as possible on secondary roads where there are lower speed limits, a lot less traffic and much more to see. I guess that has been an experience for you and now you can phone Shirley and tell her all about it."

I breathed a huge sigh of relief when Charles indicated and left the motorway. He stopped at a filling station and then he followed the signs for "Hillview Restaurant" .

Chapter 50

As we went up a driveway lined with daffodils, crocuses and tulips, I got my first glimpse of the restaurant. It was set in the most tranquil surroundings looking over miles of unspoiled countryside. .

"It's beautiful," I said.
"I think you will like it. I have been here several times before"

But before Charles could say any more, we were welcomed into a wide foyer where a young girl in a smart black and white uniform beckoned us through and led us up a small flight of steps towards the dining room where we were met by a tall, smartly dressed waiter. The table was covered with a crisp white linen tablecloth with a spray of forsythia as a centrepiece. The waiter pulled out my chair and as I sat down, he placed my napkin on my lap. Charles sat opposite me with a warm smile.

"It's a beautiful place," I said when the waiter had left.

We had hardly settled in our seats before a wine-waiter came to take our orders. I decided to try one of their red wines but let Charles make the choice. "A small glass of wine for me. I'm driving," Charles said, "and a jug of iced water."

Then the waiter passed us menus and Charles seemed quite impressed with my confidence in choosing the different courses. "You know quite a lot about food," he smiled at me across the table. "Well I should. I have worked in the kitchen for fifteen years. And don't forget I always helped Meg serve in the parlour for the board of governors."

"Yes I do remember. And you both did a splendid job."

Other diners sat in quiet whispers. So different from "The Manor". Did I miss the clanging and smashing and shouting, the arguments and fights? Maybe I did, just a little, but this was so peaceful with heavenly views out across the lake and over the mountains. The conversation with Charles was easy. We were both relaxed and I was able to speak freely. He had become a great friend and had always been a good listener.

"I was not always a free woman. I thank you for my freedom."

"Yours has been a life of courage and I know you have suffered unbearable torments. Kathy I hope we have done our best for you..." he paused.

"You have always done your best for me and for all the other patients," I said.

"And you know if it does not work out you will always have a job and accommodation in Matron's quarters, free board and lodgings and a salary and able to go down into the town to do the shopping."

After the meal, Charles dropped a generous tip on the table and we walked out into the spring sunshine. Before getting back in the car, we stood by the side of a pond in the garden, looking at the fountains and watching the swans glide by.

"I'm adrift from reality," I thought. "I have taken a step forward in time and I now have a curious sensation of looking out on someone else's world."

Charles always seemed to be able to read my thoughts, "It's a new beginning, a turn in the road, a path into another life. Good luck. But remember you're not alone."

"Thank you Charles for the journey, for all your help and for the meal. The food was delicious."

"But you will be back here again. This is half way between....." he laughed. "I was going to say between the old life and the new but I don't know quite how to put it. I know you have had so many different takes on the subject."

"Between madness and sanity," I said. "Yes I would love to come back here one day." We drove along, relaxed and enjoying the beautiful countryside. I suddenly gasped as familiar territory came into view. "We're almost there," I said. "I recognise every twist and turn of these narrow roads."

As we rounded the last bend, the light shining into the car windows was warm and golden. The village had appeared so small, just a dent in the landscape but here we were now at the wooden gates at the bottom of the drive. Charles drove slowly between the lines of ancient fruit trees and shrubs.

"Stop! I said," For a moment I felt I couldn't go any further. I held my face in my hands and Charles waited. "You take as long as you need," he said. I took several deep breaths and then told Charles to go on slowly. The farmhouse was set deep in a hollow at the bottom of the drive beneath a tumble of spring flowers with the last traces of bluebells beneath the trees. I was experiencing a sense of coming home but somehow I was filled with fear and trepidation.

Rosie was the first to greet me as I stepped from the car. Her chest swelled with emotion and her eyes were wet as she held me in a long embrace. We just stood there, clinging to each other and I cried with the tears of a lifetime.

"Welcome home," she said at last. "You have come back to your family and friends. This is where you belong."

It was a strange new world. For all those years, I had been in the wilderness and here I was back where it all began. Then Rosie turned around and introduced Paul, her husband and their children Molly and Daniel. More greetings were exchanged and the children seemed to be at a loss to know what was going on. "Come and give your Auntie Kathy a big hug," she said. I knew then that I was part of a real family again.

First they took me to my extension where I could freshen up after the journey. It was part of the main building with connecting doors which gave me a sense of security. But I had my own side entrance for my independence. I invited Charles to come in with us. This was truly a little haven. There was everything I could wish for, a blazing coal fire and one wall in my lounge was covered in books. I stopped suddenly, astounded! I couldn't believe my eyes and looked more closely. These were my books and some of Meg's, our favourite authors and were a gift from Charles and Shirley.

"How did you manage this?" I asked Charles and he smiled across at Rosie. This was such an emotional moment and he held my hand as I gazed along the spines of all my old favourites. I knew in time these would be my most cherished possessions. Then Rosie took us on a tour around the extension before we tidied ourselves up for the homecoming party in the main lounge.

"I think I'll just slip away now," Charles said.

"How can I thank you, I owe it all to you," I said.

"You owe it all to yourself, to your own courage, your endurance," he replied. "This is not goodbye. We will meet up again."

"Definitely. We must! Matron says she is going to hold on to my little room until I make my final decision."

"Well, it's all settled then."

Rosie and I accompanied Charles out my side door. "Strange how fate takes so many twists and turns," I thought. We watched as Charles started up the car and drove out the wooden gate, waving as he went. We just stood there in silence until he was out of sight.

As we walked through to the main part of the building, Aunt Dolly was there to greet me and stretched out her hands. They all welcomed me as if I was the prodigal daughter returned. The house felt strange to me, like somewhere I had visited only in a dream. It's as though nature tested me for endurance and constancy to prove whether I was good enough to return to the fold.

Chapter 51

Rosie had told me that Father Brian, the new parish priest had asked to see me and I decided to go on the first evening of my arrival.

"No, no. It's too soon. Why don't you settle in first and we will talk about it tomorrow."

"But I want to go. I want to see Tommy's grave and arrange a proper burial."

"Okay, we will phone and tell him we are on the way. I will drive you down to Father Brian myself," Rosie said "as soon as you are ready". Rosie decided to visit a friend a few doors away from the presbytery and said I could join them later. This was going to be one of the most difficult visits. I went to see Father Brian in fear and trembling, not hoping or expecting anything. They would close ranks against me, cover up. This place carried so much sadness for me. I almost changed my mind as I was about to ring the door bell, thinking back to the evils of Fr. Lynch and all those who had been responsible for my unlawful incarceration.

But I received a friendly greeting. Father Brian held my hand and looked at me with a warmth and kindness in his eyes. His old sheepdog wagged his tail and waddled back to lie in his basket.

"Welcome home Kathy. Rosie has told me everything and I am so glad you came. This must be difficult for you. I want to apologise on behalf of my fellow clergyman who was capable of such evil. We don't want to go into all that now but the church has a lot to answer for."

I wasn't expecting such understanding and burst into tears. He took my hand. "It's not just the church," I said through my sobs, "but my family too."

"All those who should have been loving you, protecting you. May God forgive them and may justice be done." Father Brian bowed his head.

"Come in," he said and welcomed me into a cosy sitting room where a warm fire was blazing in the grate. A small coffee table was set with two cups and saucers and a plate of cakes. "Do you want to help me make the tea?" he said. "I don't like leaving you alone as I know this place must have many sad memories for you."

"Thank you," I said "for putting me at my ease. To be honest I was dreading this interview but I knew I had to do it as soon as possible."

"It's not an interview," Brian laughed. "Friends among friends. And I must admit I was nervous myself. I didn't know what to expect. You have put me so much at my ease." These were strange words coming from a priest.

We talked a bit about 'The Manor'. "I had friends there, friends I will never forget who helped turn my life around." I didn't say any more. I knew I would have lots more opportunities to chat with Brian. He had already gained my affections and my respect. I could see he believed in me and had real concern for my future.

"How about you. Do you like it here?" I asked. I was amazed by my own confidence. I could never have spoken with an adult like that before Meg had helped me to face people and to believe in myself.

"I have been here for eighteen months," he replied. "Before that I was a curate in a small town in southeast Somerset and before that I was at a theological college in London. Believe it or not, before that I was a carpenter, see my handiwork," he pointed to some book shelves. I knew instantly that I had found a new friend. He had put me at my ease. In many ways he reminded me of Meg. Life was going to be good after all. I wanted to tell him about the bookshelves I had made and the library and Meg teaching me to read and a whole lot of other things. But all that could wait.

"Every morning at 7.30 I take my dog out for a walk. We walk to the church where I say my prayers, offering the day to God and asking him to guide me and be with me in everything I do as he has promised he will. Sometimes it is just me and old Shep but often I am joined by a handful of parishioners. Then there is the usual admin, dealing with the day's post and answering the phone. Some mornings I visit the hospital and the hospice."

"In the afternoons I usually go around the parish on my bike with Shep at my heels to visit some of the sick and housebound. It helps us to keep fit. I enjoy the fresh air and exercise and it's easier to see people and for them to see me. My bike is good because I can get around quite quickly on it but I can also stop if I want and walk along chatting with someone. So in a way that is how I cope with the day-to-day running of the parish. So that's it. And how about you? Have you got any plans?"

"I will stay with Rosie for a while until Tommy has a proper burial and then write to Matron and take it from there. I will come back another day and talk about Tommy."

"Of course you will. I think we will be seeing a lot of each other."

Kathy Lavelle

Chapter 52

When we got back home, Paul was sitting watching football on TV. He jumped up and put on the kettle and we sat there for some time going over the events of the day. "You must be exhausted," he said.

"Yes a bit," I said. "But Rosie has promised to take me out for a little fresh air before we turn in."
We went to our rooms and changed into something more practical. Rosie appeared in blue jeans and a white blouse gathered with a string and I wore jeans and a check shirt which had been a parting gift from Matron. We could not stop looking at each other until she grabbed my hand and pulled me out the door, into the garden. There was nothing to be heard except the odd animal noise. The traffic and the village seemed a million miles away.

I held onto Rosie's hand and breathed in the scent of home where the soft murmur of the wind mingled with the farmyard noises as we walked towards the bright green grass behind the house until we reached the narrow waterfall bouncing down the rock wall, its spray a shimmering rainbow in the long dying rays of the sun

The gentle breeze was beckoning softly from the river as we walked along in silence, enjoying the peace of the night. I no longer felt any pain. Everything around seemed to fill me with tranquillity. The gentle breeze caressed my face. Winter had turned to spring. The wind of the previous night had diminished to a gentle whisper and the river gurgled out there where the sun had now set and the dark sky went up and up forever and there were hundreds and thousands of stars.

I remembered one of Shirley's favourite songs on the old gramophone, "If all of the stars were a million guitars." I stood there in awe. Was Shirley out there looking up at the sky? What was she thinking? I wondered if she would even come to visit me here. But she said. "I will never step outside these doors again, not after the way people out there have treated me. Meg had used exactly the same words. I wouldn't be seeing Meg again but she is here with me, always in my heart.

We walked down the hillside with only the lights from the house to guide our steps. Paul had already gone to bed and we sat there and talked and talked into the small hours.

"It's been a long day," I said.

"And an eventful one," Rosie said. "Welcome home Kathy."

The events of the day were spinning around in my head as I lay down in my cosy bed that first night. Images from my dreams and perceptions were all mixed together in my mind. I thought of Meg, Matron, Shirley and Charles and Father Brian.

Chapter 53

The next morning as dawn was beginning to seep across the horizon, Rosie and I stepped out on the hillside, walking hand-in-hand in an easy silence. Everything seemed strange, greener and smaller, a softer landscape. The rocks had shrunken but so much was unchanged, cows in the fields, the stream, the trees and the heather.

I wandered ahead of Rosie and let my thoughts run. I was back again in that quiet place with the noise of the water over stones, the broad, warm rocks. I heard a rumble of wheels across the way where we used to play. It was so peaceful everywhere, it didn't feel real, like the world had stopped spinning. As I reached the brow of the hill, Michael's house was just visible in the distance with smoke curling out of the chimney. I had Michael's promise in my mind but things were very different now.

Just then Rosie caught up with me and interrupted my thoughts. "Michael has been out since dawn," she pointed towards the lambing shed and at that moment a figure appeared on the horizon. "There he is," she said, pointing in his direction. I could see him now. He had a small bundle in his arms. He came down the hill towards us.

Rosie greeted him and said, "I'll be heading back to the house now. See you later" and she rushed across the heather before she had finished speaking.

I would have known him immediately although he was a good deal sturdier and handsome. I could really see that now. His shyness had gone and he didn't look anything like that boy anymore. The physical nature of his work had kept him in good shape but he was a bit heavier than he had been at sixteen. Everything about him seemed different. Michael, the boy, had disappeared and in his place this handsome man. Had I changed as much? Well yes of course I must have. I was a girl of sixteen and now I am a woman, fifteen years older.

We stood in silence for a while, half a lifetime in the space between us. I felt something twist inside me but it was all so long ago I could no longer be sure what was pleasure and what was fear. We stood watching each other. It was as if we were so close I could feel his breath around me. I had lived so differently those last fifteen years and I really was scared now but his smile lit up both our faces and his eyes looked into mine, studying me all the time and bringing back my confidence. It was as if I'd expected time to stand still. We were quiet for a time, looking at each other, united by a thought, knowing instinctively that we understood each other after all these years.

Everything was proceeding as usual, as though nothing had happened. I waited for him to speak. I remembered his voice was always tentative and mild. I approached him gently.

"Welcome home," he said.

"Thanks," I took his outstretched hand.

"It must have been very difficult for you," he paused. "Life hasn't been easy for me either," he said and I saw tears in his eyes.

"I know. Rosie told me everything."

"First there was Joanna. Only two years ago....." he paused. "And then the problems on the farm....." But he stopped there. There was so much to say. A lifetime of telling and asking. Catching up on years of living and missed opportunities.

Meg had warned me against regretting what might have been. "We'll never know," she said.

He still had the little bundle, snugly wrapped and cradled in his arms. I thought at first it was a stillborn lamb wrapped in a twist of old sacking. "I need to find a home for this poor little creature. His mother died after the birth" And suddenly the baby lamb opened his eyes. There was something about the way he lay so still in Michael's arms.

"I'll take care of him," I said and I took the lamb still wrapped in his bit of sack and held him snugly against my own body. I touched the damp spot of nose and fell in love with him on the spot. For the first time, I felt I was really home and that time had stood still. "I'll take him back to our own lambing shelter," I said and Michael just smiled. It was as if we had never been apart. He took a small bottle of ewe's milk from this pocket and handed it to me. Something of the old flame flickered up in me. I remember those first nights when we worked by the light of an oil lamp in the barn at lambing time.

"Will you be staying then?" he asked.

I hesitated for a while. "At least until this little chap is fighting fit and leaping over those rocks." I smiled and Michael looked out over the moor.

That evening, I went back for some more milk to where Michael was working in the lambing shed. A shimmer of raindrops sprang out, covering the sun and arching a rainbow across the sky. As the light turned to dusk that evening, I think I could for the moment see through Michael's body and soul. The last rays of sunset had faded as we stood and stared across the brown water like we used to do fifteen years ago, and at that moment a nightingale sang.

We followed the small path trampled in the grass and suddenly there it was, a widening in the river, a vast expanse of water. Willows swung their fringes and weed swayed, dancing and caressing the water. I put my hand into the water and my thoughts drifted with it, as I stood beside Michael again. I felt like running with the wind in my hair like I used to do so long ago. I wanted to stand on the bridge and listen to the owl. Michael walked with me along the narrow sheep path and through the trees towards the house.

He thanked me for taking the lamb as we stood in the gateway shaking hands. He leaned over and for a second I wondered if he might kiss me but instead he brushed his fingers lightly across my cheek. "Welcome back," he said again.

When I turned and walked towards the house, I felt his eyes following me. I had returned to life and taken my customary place, reunited with Michael and Rosie and ready to open the door to my new life.

I stood and watched as Michael walked back across the purple heather on the slender sheep trails dipping away to invisibility in the darkening sky.

The landscape was vast and endless and free.

Kathy Lavelle